CAMILLE STYLES
entertaining

CAMILLE STYLES

entertaining

INSPIRED GATHERINGS & EFFORTLESS STYLE

Photographs by Buff Strickland

𝒲𝓂

WILLIAM MORROW

An Imprint of HarperCollins *Publishers*

CAMILLE STYLES ENTERTAINING. Copyright © 2014 by Camille Styles, Inc. All rights reserved. Printed in the United States of America. No part of this book may be used or reproduced in any manner whatsoever without written permission except in the case of brief quotations embodied in critical articles and reviews. For information address HarperCollins Publishers, 195 Broadway, New York, NY 10007.

HarperCollins books may be purchased for educational, business, or sales promotional use. For information please e-mail the Special Markets Department at SPSales@harpercollins.com.

FIRST EDITION

Designed by Trina Bentley
Photographs by Buff Strickland

Library of Congress Cataloging-in-Publication Data has been applied for.

ISBN 978-0-06-229727-3

14 15 16 17 18   OV/RRD   10 9 8 7 6 5 4 3 2 1

TO ADAM, MY OTHER HALF, WHO GIVES ME THE COURAGE TO DO WHAT I LOVE. AND TO MY DARLING PHOEBE, WHO MAKES EVERY DAY CAUSE FOR CELEBRATION. THE TWO OF YOU MAKE LIFE INFINITELY ENTERTAINING.

CONTENTS

SPRING

SUMMER

We could see the excitement
as their faces registered
that this was a kick-off-
your-heels-and-break-out-the-
tequila kind of party!

CELEBRATE THE EVERYDAY

On a recent sticky-hot July evening in Austin, my husband, Adam, and I invited a few of his friends from work to join us for a casual dinner on our back patio. We wanted to keep the vibe laid-back and fun while marking a big milestone for their company, so I appointed a "shorts and sandals" dress code and set out to infuse the occasion with a few simple but surprising details that guaranteed it would be a night to remember.

Thirty Mexican prayer candles, five platters of build-your-own-tacos, four pitchers of frozen margaritas, and one donkey piñata later, we had all the makings of a south-of-the-border fiesta. Adam cranked up the mariachi tunes on the speakers, and as our guests showed up (perhaps expecting just another "work dinner"), we could see the excitement as their faces registered that this was a kick-off-your-heels-and-break-out-the-tequila kind of party!

That unforgettable evening perfectly illustrates my secret to modern, stress-free entertaining: keep the focus on just a handful of details that pack a major punch and leave a lasting impression in guests' minds. It all starts with creating the *vision* for your party: the overarching theme that will drive all other decisions and serve as the launching pad for the creative details that make a party unforgettable. The vision will determine the look and feel of your invitation, decor, items on a menu, guests' attire, drinks that are poured, and music that's played.

But don't think for a second that I wait around for life's big milestones to delve into my inspiration files and come up with a great idea for a party. Even if it's "just" a cozy weekend dinner at home, I love to take a few moments to craft a vision that will elevate a normal night into something fun and unexpected. When the weather's nice, I may throw a swath of white linen on our patio table and place a scattering of glass votives and a few branches clipped from our lemon tree in the center and then set each place with my favorite handmade ceramic dishes, textured linen napkins, and stemless wineglasses for a look that's completely unfussy yet transports us to a wine country setting for the evening. Northern Cali cuisine like grilled fish with seasonal vegetables, chilled glasses of Sauvignon Blanc, and a couple scoops of sorbet are in keeping with the vibe . . . and, just as important, make for almost zero prep time in the kitchen. These small gestures are the spice of life, and they're at the heart of my philosophy to celebrate the everyday, living each moment as something worth remembering.

When I got married, I decided not to register for special-occasion china, instead choosing beautiful dishes that could grace the dinner table nightly. I don't wait for parties to break out my

favorite table linens, and neither should you! After all, throwing them in the washing machine at the end of the evening takes very little effort, and the enjoyment gained from sitting down to a beautiful table far outweighs it. At some point in my life, I realized that all the "stuff" we own is temporary—it can be lost or broken, and as the saying goes, you can't take it with you!

So while I'm not always successful at it, I do my best to seize the day and let the beautiful items I own bring me joy *right this minute* instead of waiting for a "worthy" opportunity. We all deserve to be surrounded by beauty, and if something breaks, it can be fixed; if it's lost, it can be replaced. Even if you're spending an evening solo eating Chinese takeout, set the table with *real* dishes and glassware, pour yourself a glass of wine, and savor a good meal. It's moments like these that set us on a path toward living the life we dream of—a life in which we're respecting our bodies with nourishing food, nurturing our souls by making time for our passions, engaging our senses with beauty, and expressing our love to family and friends by inviting them to create memories together.

There's no good reason to wait for another day to start living like you want to live. Think of this book as your guide to the simple details and creative shortcuts that make everyday moments feel special, even in the midst of our busy, schedule-packed lives. After reading it, I hope you'll be inspired to invite a few friends over, and instead of slaving away at the stove all day, get creative by thinking of a few fun details that'll make it special and leave you feeling energized and excited when the doorbell rings. "Entertaining" can happen with 100 people or just one—it's really just a state of mind that says, "Today is worthy of celebrating. Let's make it fun!"

Camille

1

FINDING BEAUTY

>>>>>>>>>> IN THE DETAILS <<<<<<<<<<

For as long as I can remember, I've sought out—and delighted in—beauty in the details. As a little girl, I collected stacks of binders full of images that inspired me, visited art museums with my parents (falling in love with the great Impressionists), and sketched and memorized the names of all my favorite flowers. As I got older, I discovered that beauty could just as easily be found in a recipe where all the components came together in perfect harmony, a song whose lyrics seemed to speak directly into the heart, and best of all, in the moments shared with my family and friends that left me feeling cherished and cared for. I developed a passion for seeking out these moments of beauty in everyday life, and though I had no idea at the time what it would look like, I knew I wanted my life's

work to somehow involve creating beauty for myself and others to enjoy.

My first real job after college was at a catering company in Austin. It was a demanding and sometimes stressful role, but I couldn't have asked for a better education in event planning and production, menu design, and staying calm in the face of immense pressure (and sometimes even potential disaster!). I did it all: served wedding cake to five hundred people, came up with a quick solution when the power to the portable toilets went out, even passed hors d'oeuvres at swanky cocktail parties when we were short on waiters. I developed the ability to think on my feet, the gift of calming the occasional bridezilla, and a team-player mentality that taught me no job was too small or too menial.

Camille

I really wholeheartedly loved working in catering, even embracing the long hours that came with it, but eventually I got a great opportunity to plan corporate events for one of my clients at an advertising agency. This job was also life changing, though in ways I could never have foreseen. It was there I met Adam, the agency's cofounder, and a few years later we were married (and now we have a one-year-old daughter, Phoebe!). He was my biggest advocate from the start, giving me the confidence, courage, and business advice I'd need to strike out on my own at age twenty-five and launch my own planning company, Camille Styles Events.

As a young entrepreneur, I had to learn a lot about starting and running a small business, marketing (with zero budget), and working with an incredibly wide range of personality types. I was raised with a strong belief in great customer service, and working from a mentality that the client's always right has served me well. But the biggest lesson I learned came from observing hosts and hostesses, who were often so stressed out and anxious about their upcoming events that by the time their party rolled around, they just wanted to hurry up and get it over with!

I knew in my gut that there had to be a better way. I mean, the whole point of parties is that they're supposed to be *fun*, right? Yet so often fun didn't even factor into these parties— they were more about impressing their guests and stressing over whether everything went off perfectly (including things completely out of anyone's control, like the weather!). As I worked to build my clientele, I also decided to launch a blog, CamilleStyles.com, as a personal outlet for creativity as well as a portfolio of sorts to attract clients. This core vision of making parties fun and stress-free became my battle cry to harried hosts everywhere, and I made it a personal goal to help my clients, as well as my blog readers, rediscover the beauty, meaning, and sheer deliciousness that make hosting gatherings worth our time and effort.

When Adam and I married, I relished in making our home into a haven, and like so many newlyweds, we began to entertain much more frequently. Even when it was just the two of us, we set the table, lit candles, and cooked something delicious—and suddenly a night at home was elevated to a moment worthy of savoring and remembering. It made me realize that I wanted my website to be a place where readers could not only find ideas for life's big celebrations but also get inspired to infuse beauty into their daily lives through the food they made, the rooms they designed, the outfits they wore, and the way they pampered themselves.

Flash-forward four years, and I'll be honest: sometimes I have to pinch myself when I wake up in the morning and spend my "workday" immersed in all the things that I love. Sure, just like any other job it has its unglamorous moments (accounting, anyone?), but to browse my favorite blogs, interview fascinating and stylish people, flip through books on art and design in the name of research, and most of all, challenge myself to continue being creative every single day? I wouldn't trade it for the world.

Within these pages is a combination of practical wisdom from my years spent planning events professionally, jaw-dropping images that are born from my lifelong pursuit of beauty, and loads of advice and inspiration from some of the most creative and interesting people I know, all of them total experts in their fields. There are also lots of tidbits on how I organize my home, look my best when I'm short on time, feed my family deliciously, and really just live my life in the very best way I can. I hope this book encourages each of you to wake up every morning with a desire to engage the senses—to open your eyes fully to the beauty that surrounds you. Instead of "saving" your loveliest things for some day in the future, I want you to set your tables with your best dishes (go ahead and use the linen napkins, too), wear the dress that makes you feel great (even if your destination is the grocery store), and buy the freshest, most bursting-with-flavor seasonal ingredients at the market to inspire tonight's dinner. A great bottle of wine wouldn't hurt, either.

I love the term that psychologists use for those times when you're living in the moment, utterly immersed in your present activity. It's called *flow*, and while the experience is different for everyone depending on their unique abilities and passions, the common denominator is an experience of joy and serenity. So remember: everything here is simply a launching pad for your own creativity. As you walk through your day, watch for that inspiring cue—maybe it's a vivid color or a surprising flavor combination—that captures your imagination and invites you to create something uniquely your own. Then dive right into life and express *your* creativity at its best—after all, nothing's more beautiful than your truest self, shining its brightest!

fall

"always a
...lish veled, a bit
broken down"

2

SIGHTS, SOUNDS, AND TASTES OF FALL

This morning, as Adam, Phoebe, and I headed out for our daily walk to the coffee shop, we watched the neighborhood kids boarding the bus for their first day of school. Though it's been years since I've donned a backpack, I was immediately filled with that sense of giddy excitement that only a new school year can bring. While every season has its own story of new beginnings, for me, fall has always symbolized the ultimate in fresh starts, bursting with the promise of shiny red apples and infinite potential for the coming months. This is the season of trees erupting in colorful splendor and scents of cinnamon and cider wafting from the kitchen, the time when I take stock of my wardrobe and invest in that beautiful cashmere sweater or leather handbag that I'll keep for years, when evenings return indoors and dinners on the terrace become cozy suppers by the fire.

My favorite fall celebrations include autumnal flavors and a few rustic touches, and this season is devoted in part to those treasured rituals that usher in the cooler months. And what better place to start than Thanksgiving, the ultimate in autumn tradition?

Though you've got to love a holiday dedicated to family and a table groaning with platters of delicious food, there's no

Camille

question that Thanksgiving can bring its own set of hostess anxieties (cooking the turkey! perfecting the piecrust!). Though I now consider it one of my favorite days of the year, the very first Thanksgiving I ever hosted was *far* from stress-free.

Adam and I had just gotten married, and we (misguidedly) decided it would be a good idea to invite both sides of our families to celebrate Thanksgiving in our nine-hundred-square-foot bungalow. The night before the feast, as we carefully removed the giblets from the inside of our turkey, we noticed it still seemed a little frozen in the middle, but in our total inexperience, we assumed all would be fine and it would be thawed by the next day. Adam was planning to fry a turkey (for the first time, I might add), and we'd stocked up on a brand-new turkey fryer and vats of cooking oil just for the occasion.

In the morning, our families arrived and we all got to prepping in our tiny kitchen. I tasked my younger sister, Molly, with the jobs of peeling potatoes and cleaning lettuce, and—though I'm not laying blame—*something* off-limits must have dropped into the garbage disposal, because before we knew it the sink was clogged . . . and since everything was connected to the same drainage system, the only toilet in the house was, too. For the next couple of hours, our guests shuttled to the neighborhood coffee shop for bathroom breaks as Adam and my dad tried to fix the issue while waiting for the emergency plumber to arrive.

Finally, it was time to get the turkey in the deep fryer. All the men went outside to watch the action, and Adam set his watch for the optimal cooking time. Of course, our dads, in all their years of turkey-cooking wisdom, convinced him to leave it in *a little longer* than planned *just in case* . . . and several minutes later they pulled out a burned-to-a-crisp turkey. As we sat down to carve the blackened beast, my father-in-law reached in, and much to our dismay, pulled out a small plastic bag. Apparently, due to the partially frozen state of the turkey's interior the night before, I'd mistakenly left it in the cavity, where it had fried right along with the rest of the bird. Suffice it to say that, at that particular Thanksgiving feast, the side dishes were the stars of the show.

We've hosted Thanksgiving at our house every year since, and each one gets a little more seamless and, yes, delicious. Every time we gather around the table, someone inevitably brings up that first Thanksgiving that we shared together, and we all laugh about the completely unforgettable day. And I'd bet that we're all secretly giving thanks for a bigger house with multiple bathrooms and a perfectly golden, juicy, *roasted* turkey.

HERE'S HOW I CONNECT WITH ALL THE SENSES TO USHER IN THE FALL SEASON:

TEXTURE.

Cozy cashmere, nubby wool, and worn-in flannel are so welcome to the touch when the air turns cool. At home, this is the time when all my energy goes into making our living spaces as inviting and comfortable as possible. I lay down rugs to warm bare feet, toss a few plush throw pillows in varying textures on the couch, and place an oversize cable-knit throw over an armchair that just *begs* for someone to curl up and take a nap.

SCENT.

In the fall, I renew my nightly bathtime ritual that's a much-anticipated transition from the busyness of the workday to a serene, bedtime frame of mind. If you're not usually into baths, I'd encourage you to give it a shot! The mere act of sinking into a hot sudsy tub relaxes the muscles and clears the mind of daily stressors to make room for calm and serenity. To make it the ultimate sensory experience, I burn a lavender candle and place a few drops of rose essential oil into the water. Postbath, I wrap up in an extra plush towel and moisturize from head to toe with a rich body butter that smells like honeysuckle. It's an at-home ritual that will give your local spa a run for its money.

COLOR.

Turning leaves, plaid scarves, and market stalls piled high with squash and countless varieties of apples: these iconic symbols of fall get me in the mood for a rich palette in shades of amethyst and pumpkin. On the table, I bring out my stoneware plates in earthy shades of taupe, lay down flax-hued napkins, and light candles that cast a golden glow when darkness begins to descend earlier each evening. In my wardrobe, I gravitate toward an organic-feeling palette of cream, taupe, and black, with a few jewel-toned pieces in the mix to add vibrancy. And now is most definitely the season to experiment with more drama in the makeup department. A ruby lip, emerald eye shadow, or kohl-lined lash (though please, not all at once) brings a welcome sense of polish after the barefaced days of summer.

TASTE.

How do I love fall cooking? Let me count the apple-pie-scented ways . . . Long before the first hints of cooler weather arrive, I'm already fantasizing about platters of roasted butternut squash with sage, hearty grain salads studded with dried fruit, and juicy turkey with glistening skin. I'm finally ready to leave behind the fresh berries and light sorbets of summer in favor of apple crisp baked in cast-iron skillets and my mom's famous pecan pie. In fact, it's these food rituals that really epitomize autumn celebrations for me. Usher in the season by making a few tried-and-true recipes that smell and taste like total comfort. And why not use it as an excuse to reconnect with people who are back in town after summertime travels? Invite a group to join you for an early fall dinner; there's no better way to say "welcome home."

3

SETTING THE FALL TABLE

As alfresco dinners become a relic of summertime and every passing day gets a bit shorter than the one before, my thoughts turn to cozying up the dining room and making the table an inviting spot where everyone slows down and lingers awhile. It's the place where our family gathers during the week to talk and catch up about the events of the day . . . and where our friends gather on weekends for long pancake brunches or dinners with red wine and bowls full of pasta. And of course, the table is the *real* star of the show on Thanksgiving, when it's transformed into a cornucopia of delicious food and everyone gathers around for the biggest feast of the year. For fall's table setting, I was inspired by the jewel-toned richness of wine country: trailing vines dripping with grapes and the unexpected interplay of rustic textures and ornate detailing.

Camille

PALETTE.

Amethyst, ivy, cream, charcoal.

LINENS.

It was love at first sight when I laid eyes on this pale gray linen tablecloth inscribed with trailing vines, flowers, and birds. It has a vintage family-heirloom quality that feels just right for fall, and its neutral palette is the perfect backdrop for linen napkins in a rich shade of amethyst.

CENTERPIECE.

My friend and floral designer, Elizabeth Lewis, creative director of the Nouveau Romantics, filled a low wooden bowl with flowers in every shade of purple, ranging from burgundy to pink; it echoed the other tabletop details without being overly matchy. Oak-leaf hydrangeas make a beautiful focal flower with their unique conical shape, and clematis, jasmine vines, scabiosa, astrantia, and ranunculus completed the design. When creating a low, wide arrangement, we always start by balling up chicken wire and attaching it to the inside of the vase using floral tape for a structure that will stabilize the flowers as you start adding them. To create this horizontal shape, think about going "long" with the arrangement—letting vines trail horizontally and onto the tabletop itself.

PLACE SETTINGS.

On a trip to San Francisco a few years ago, I discovered Heath Ceramics, a Bay Area–based pottery company, and became obsessed with the beauty and simplicity of their dinnerware. I added these white coupe plates to my collection and have since incorporated them into just about every style of table design you can imagine. Proof that it always pays to invest in a versatile set of white dishes! Here I've paired the plates with vintage silverware and delicate etched glassware that was passed down from my great-grandmother.

THE DETAILS.

I tied a rich velvet ribbon around each set of vintage flatware for a five-second touch that feels more modern than napkin rings and makes for an effortless way to attach a calligraphied place card to each setting. The napkins are made from a beautiful bolt of amethyst linen fabric that I cut to size and left unhemmed, and an oversize wood-topped decanter placed on the table is a wine-country-esque showpiece that's as beautiful as it is functional.

SOURCES

Floral design: The Nouveau Romantics
Calligraphy: Antiquaria
Props: Loot Vintage Rentals
Tabletop pieces: Anthropologie

4

FINDING AND HOLDING ON TO INSPIRATION

From the time I was five years old, my mother discovered she could keep me endlessly entertained with a stack of old magazines, a blank notebook, and a glue stick. I'd spend hours working on my collages, an early form of what later became my inspiration files—one of the most important tools in my creative process. There was something so energizing about flipping through the magazines and ripping out whatever caught my eye, for no other reason than I found it beautiful. Maybe it was a certain shade of blue or the way a model carried herself or the pattern of a tablecloth . . . but something in the image told me that I needed to hold on to it and store it away for the future.

Years later, I'm every bit as obsessed with finding and keeping images that thrill me, and many of my favorites have helped shape all different aspects of my life, from fashion to food to interior

design. Today folders on my computer are dedicated to ideas for future projects and parties, and a huge cork board hangs in the center of my office, providing a constant source of creative stimulation (and eye candy).

The process of continually developing my personal style always starts with discovering inspiration that excites me and stirs something up in my soul. Of course, this can come from countless sources besides magazines and websites; some of my favorite ideas were sparked by something as unexpected as the shape of a perfume bottle on my makeup table or the handmade stoneware used at a great restaurant in LA. Looking for your own visual inspiration is a lifelong journey, so cast a wide net and don't forget that it can be found wherever you go (which makes every minute of life an adventure, don't you think?).

Camille

So how do I approach the process of finding, organizing, and translating inspiration into a highly personal style that reflects who I am? For starters, I take photos wherever I go. When I spot a woman wearing an outfit I love, read an innovative restaurant menu, or notice an eye-catching typeface in an ad, I pull out my phone and snap away (best to ask permission if you're photographing a person, though!). I'll often e-mail the photo to myself with a note in the subject line about why I loved it—and then, once back at home, I'll save it on my computer to be accessed later. Magazines are obviously a rich source for beautiful ideas, but don't disregard catalogs from fashion or home brands that you love: I often flip through West Elm and Anthropologie catalogs to see how their teams set the table or style a bedroom nightstand. When my heart beats a little faster on a certain page, I carefully cut it out and scan a high-res image so I always have a digital copy saved. Of course, you can go low-tech if that's more your thing! Pinning images onto a cork board, gluing into a notebook, or storing them in file folders near your desk can be every bit as effective. The key is to keep them in a spot where you can find them when you need them.

I also subscribe to blogs across lots of different categories and start most days by scrolling through new posts. It's amazing how reading about food can spark an idea for a dinner party theme, which then dictates the flowers I'm going to buy for the table—but that's just how inspiration works! The creative process is meandering and unpredictable, and when I allow myself to follow an idea down a path but I'm not sure where it might lead, delightful bursts of inspiration strike when I least suspect them.

It's no surprise that travel provides some of the richest opportunities for inspiration. When Adam and I started the process of building our house three years ago, we brought a scrapbook to that first meeting with our architect that contained snapshots from our honeymoon on the Amalfi Coast. We'd come away so inspired by the white stucco buildings, stone planters overflowing with colorful bougainvillea, and most of all, the deep blue of the Mediterranean Sea that we longed to re-create a taste of that same beauty in the design of our future home. Years later, it makes me smile to wake up each morning and push back the sheer white curtains that remind me so much of the ones in our beachside hotel room.

It's worth noting that inspiration files can and *should* include images that are pure fantasy. So what if your finances don't allow for exact reproduction of that Italian villa you fell in love with online? Maybe you could create a similar look in your garden by planting mounds of rosemary bushes or a couple of citrus trees. The inspiration you gather from all these varied sources might be literal (spotting the perfect paint color for your dining room) or more abstract (reading *The Great Gatsby*, then throwing a dinner party with a Jazz Age vibe; seeing a painting that inspires you to redo your bedroom with an Impressionist feel). Don't overthink the process: if you love an image, save it, and you may realize only later how it helped to shape your aesthetic.

Every once in a while, I take stock of my inspiration files and sort through the images, searching for the common thread in color scheme, texture—even an overall feeling of energy or serenity. This is the time for ruthless editing: if I can't remember why I saved a photo or feel like it no longer "fits," I toss it.

Your style and tastes *will* inevitably change, and I find it best to keep only the things that inspire you now. This is also when I consider which descriptive words best convey the feeling behind my collection (natural? glamorous? simple? colorful?), because honing in on such a description (mine—at least for now—is "classic and understated with a dash of bohemian") allows me to filter through all the options out there and focus on what's really "me." It also keeps me from trying to cram too many disconnected ideas into one party, room, or outfit. Whether I'm considering a new pair of shoes or making some updates to my living room, I can always refer back to my files and think about my personal style description, helping me stay true to who I am and what I really love.

Although it can be helpful to divide up your files and tear sheets by project, searching for inspiration doesn't need to wait for a home remodel or big event. It's really about a way of experiencing the world with your eyes wide open, always expecting to discover something beautiful. And what to do if you're not sure *what* inspires you? Practice looking for fresh ideas wherever you find yourself: notice the subtle genius in great books or movies, allow yourself to be moved by a favorite piece of art, savor a new taste and store it away for future experimentation in the kitchen. Get ready for a whole new adventure—one in which your heart beats a little faster and the senses are awakened in an entirely new way.

5

LIVING WITH FLOWERS

Flowers cast an intoxicating spell, turning a simple room into one brimming with romance, a pretty table into something extraordinary. Growing up, I'd help my mom plant cutting gardens full of zinnias, bachelor buttons, daisies, and sunflowers, and in summer we'd head into our magical garden armed with clippers, returning with armfuls of stems to fill the earthenware pitchers my mom placed around the house. I always said that when I grew up, I'd continue this tradition of having fresh flowers at home . . . and I do. It's an undeniable luxury but certainly not an unattainable extravagance, and over the years I've discovered a few tips that allow me to surround myself with gorgeous blooms all year long. They don't require the skills of a florist, lots of time, or wads of cash, and if you learn some basics of how to care for cut flowers, arrangements can last for a week or even longer.

Flowers are one of the most visible ways to witness the changing of the seasons and connect to the natural world in our living spaces. In this section, we'll look at how to bring autumnal flowers and foliage into our homes as we transition into cozier months. Then, on page 181, we'll breathe new life into those rooms as we freshen them up and surround ourselves with the flowering branches and feminine petals of spring. Floral designer Elizabeth Lewis will share a few industry secrets to creating beautiful arrangements for everyday life, and she created these looks for both fall and spring that feature each season's most show-stopping blooms. If you usually limit yourself to cut flowers for parties or Valentine's Day, I hope you're inspired to experience the joy of surrounding yourself with flowers—if for no other reason than taking pleasure in their innate beauty. Living with flowers helps us be fully present and embrace life's beautiful moments. We needn't wait for special occasions—*today* is worthy enough.

HOW TO BUY

Just as we take a cue from the season's ripest produce to plan our meals, why not let what's currently growing guide our flower choices? Although my flower market can order just about anything for me year-round, the advantages of buying locally include freshness (they've probably traveled a shorter distance) and a more nature-centered approach to bringing flowers into the home.

When choosing among stems, go for the blooms that aren't completely open, so they'll have a longer life once arranged. Most flowers will continue to open once cut, and part of the fun is watching your bouquets change and evolve as the buds transition to full blooms. Choose firm leaves and stems that aren't discolored.

Pick up a bunch or two of foliage to incorporate texture and color variation. Using the flower's own leaves or herbs from your garden can be really beautiful and add interest to the bouquet, and foliage is one of the most cost-effective ways to add fullness to an arrangement.

When you get home from the market, unwrap your flowers immediately and get them into water as soon as possible.

HOW TO ARRANGE

Cut stems on a diagonal using sharp scissors or a knife. The goal is to expose as much surface area on the stem as possible so that the flower can absorb the maximum amount of water.

Fill the vase with clean, lukewarm water. Use floral food (yes, it really works!) to give the flowers energy and prevent the growth of bacteria. If the vase is clear, look for a clear vase solution, or at least be sure to change the water daily. Now you're ready to start adding flowers.

Working with one stem at a time, remove all foliage that will fall below the waterline in the vase to prevent the growth of bacteria.

Build a base using foliage and/or branchy stems. Think about whether you'd like your grouping to be symmetrical or asymmetrical—this base will set the stage for the final shape.

Add focal flowers (the arrangement's pièces de résistance), using the stronger branchy stems as a foundational structure. Place these in the most visible spots so they'll be the arrangement's defining elements.

Save the most delicate flowers for the end, weaving them into the other stems to provide support. Let them be a bit more "wild"—trailing, gesticulating, and adding movement to the arrangement. I often try to create an organic look in my arrangements by thinking about how the flowers appeared when they were growing in nature. Consider a tulip's graceful curves or a vine's trailing twists and cultivate these natural "gestures" into the arrangement's shape.

HOW TO CARE FOR

Change the water daily, *especially* if you didn't add floral food to the water, to eliminate bacteria and sludge.

When flowers start to go limp, recut the stems on a forty-five-degree angle—they just might perk up again!

Discard wilted blooms immediately.

Keep your arrangement away from drafts or direct sunlight.

6

FALL IN BLOOM

NO. 1

NATURE WALK

When I was growing up, one of our family's favorite things to do on a crisp autumn day was go for a nature walk, admiring the splendor of the changing leaves, the rich display of fall flowers, and the pumpkins and gourds dotting neighbors' front porches. We'd inevitably come home with a few treasures— an unusually shaped acorn or a few especially vibrant leaves—and my mom would teach us about the different trees and flowers.

I still love a good nature walk, though now I'm often scouting out fallen branches and wild-growing berries to gather up and arrange in a vase once I'm home. There's almost no better way to celebrate the harvest season than with a bunch of branches arranged in a ceramic pitcher and placed on the mantel. To show how beautiful a walk in our own backyards can be, Liz created a dramatic arrangement that uses easy-to-find branches and leaves picked up on a woodsy stroll in October.

Camille

CHOOSE THE VESSEL.

Since this arrangement incorporates heavier branches, a vessel that has a narrow neck will hold them in place. If you're using a vessel with a wider mouth, there are a few options that will keep the branches steady:

1 | *Take a strip of chicken wire and ball it up, and then stuff it in the bottom of the base. This creates a simple structure with lots of little holes to hold each stem in place.*

2 | *Use strips of floral tape to make a grid at the mouth of the vase. Like the chicken wire, this creates narrow openings to slip each branch into, keeping the entire arrangement from toppling over to the outside of the vase.*

3 | *If the arrangement still feels a bit off-balance, try adding a few other weighty pieces to the opposite side of the vase to counterbalance and provide stability.*

CHOOSE THE FLOWERS AND FOLIAGE.

Since this design is all about taking a naturalistic approach, the exact varieties used will depend on where you live and what's easily available at a given time of year. The main thing is to use a mix of leaves (we used maple, oak, and acorn branches), flowers ('Hot Cocoa' garden roses), and fruit (persimmon and chokecherries) to give a great variety of texture. Our color palette was completely inspired by the natural gradations in the turning leaves.

PUT IT TOGETHER.

Large branches add drama and height to fill up a large space, and they should always be placed into the vase first. This creates the overall shape of the arrangement and provides a structure that will hold the more delicate pieces in place. Next, add the smaller fruiting branches (like the chokecherries) in a crisscross pattern to continue creating a foundation before adding the garden roses, the most delicate pieces. The persimmons are the unexpected little accents that finish off the arrangement and should be placed into the vase very last, like little exclamation points.

NO. 2

BERRY BRAMBLE

There's something deeply romantic about the moody shades of fall fruits, and for this darker-hued arrangement, we took our inspiration from blackberry brambles and ripe plums plucked straight from the tree. Arranged in an organic, asymmetrical shape, this grouping recalls twisting, twirling vines and is perfectly at home in a cozy reading nook or placed on a bedside table. I'd say the overall effect is about as delicious as an oozing slice of plum pie on fall's first chilly night.

CHOOSE THE VESSEL.

A petite vase provides a just-right scale for the bedside table. The narrower mouth of this one allowed us to create a lush look with fewer stems, and its black metal exterior is dramatic but simple enough not to compete with a space that boasts lots of decorative details.

CHOOSE THE FLOWERS.

At the flower market, look for flowers and foliage in shades of amethyst, fuchsia, red, and burgundy. You want to find similar berry-toned hues that have enough textural contrast to give the arrangement movement and interest. We used a variety of ranunculus, garden roses, dahlias, rose hips, plum foliage, and acorns.

PUT IT TOGETHER.

The key here is to create a loose, asymmetric shape that feels almost as though the flowers and vines are still growing in their vessel. Keep the stems tighter and lower on one side, while allowing the other side to be looser and "branchier" with a few stems reaching toward the sky. Keep in mind that dahlias (one of my favorite flowers on the planet) are a bit more delicate and will last longest if you change the water and trim the stems daily.

NO. 3

BREATH OF FRESH AIR

While pumpkin and persimmon most certainly have their place as iconic fall shades, autumn arrangements don't necessarily have to recall autumn leaves. Fall is also a time of fresh starts, and a light, bright palette perfectly conveys this clean-slate feeling. Elizabeth designed a tall, slender "breath of fresh air" arrangement using iceberg roses, white ranunculus, and trailing jasmine vines that reach outward and upward, gently taking up space and making a beautifully simple statement.

CHOOSE THE VESSEL.

A tall, narrow vase maximizes the graceful shape of these flowers, allowing them to reach up and then cascade into a gentle horizontal shape. This patinaed brass container adds richness that helps bring light-colored blooms into a more autumnal frame of mind.

CHOOSE THE FLOWERS.

We stuck with the color palette that I use most frequently when arranging flowers for my home: classic green and white. It's a combo that will work in any setting for any season, but it's far from boring when it contains exquisitely shaped roses and curling, twisting vines that add a playful touch to the composition. Since the ingredients for this arrangement are all on the thin and delicate side, you'll want to use more stems than you think you'll need in order to add fullness and create an overall look of abundance.

PUT IT TOGETHER.

When filling a tall, narrow vase, use flowers with height but that are delicate enough to not topple the entire thing over! Jasmine vines provide height and gracefulness without adding heaviness. Start by creating a shape with a few of the vines, add in the accent flowers, and then finish with a few more vines for added movement.

NO. 4

INDIAN SUMMER

There's always a touch of the bittersweet about fall, isn't there? The lazy days of summer have come and gone, and the changing seasons serve as a reminder of things past. The phrase *Indian summer* refers to a heat wave that occurs in autumn, and to me it represents a few more blissfully unexpected nights spent enjoying dinners alfresco before the true chill sends us indoors for good. In celebration of such a sentiment, Elizabeth created this simple design with a nod to the hazy, dusty glow of the Southwest. Bleached-out shades of white and wheat are awakened with touches of burgundy, perfect for lining a window or spreading down the center of a long farm table with friends and family gathered around.

CHOOSE THE VESSEL.

Since this grouping is almost stark in its simplicity, choose a vessel with strong lines that are interesting but unadorned. These brown glass bud vases resemble vintage medicine bottles that could have been on the shelves of a nineteenth-century drugstore in a dusty western town. To keep it all from looking too perfectly uniform, use vessels in a variety of heights and widths.

CHOOSE THE FLOWERS.

When working with multiple vessels that include a single variety in each of them, add interest by choosing flowers and foliage with varying height and volume. Look for shades that contrast but still complement one another, and stay within a two- or three-color palette for cohesiveness. We used cute-as-a-button 'Chocolate Cosmos,' long sheaves of wheat, and 'Charles Darwin' roses.

PUT IT TOGETHER.

It doesn't get much simpler than placing a few stems in a bud vase, making this design a foolproof option even for those who think they "can't" arrange flowers. Place the thin and delicate items (like the 'Chocolate Cosmos' and wheat) in clusters of several stems each. Since roses are full, they require only one or two stems per vase. When arranging the vessels on a tabletop or shelf, work in odd numbers for a sense of balanced asymmetry: we used three vases of roses, one vase of wheat, and one of cosmos.

FRESH CUT FLOWERS
$12.00/Bouquet

COOKING WITH THE SEASONS

I've heard it said that out of the five senses, smell is the one that most strongly evokes memories from our pasts. And while it's true that nothing takes me back to childhood quite like the scent of my mother's perfume, there's something about taste memories that recall the sights, sounds, and, most of all, *feelings* of a place in full force.

I'll never forget a certain sailboat ride that Adam and I took while on a trip to Greece a few summers ago. Upon boarding, we met our captain, Yanni, who offered us glasses of ouzo and proceeded to give us an incredible guided tour of the Mediterranean waters surrounding Santorini and its neighboring islands. We dropped anchor in an idyllic cove and dove in for a swim, and just when I thought things couldn't get any more perfect, Yanni started preparing our lunch. He pulled out a loaf of crusty bread and big chunks of salty feta made fresh on the island, then started slicing tomatoes and cucumbers he'd plucked from his garden that morning. He spread it all out on a wood chopping board, added a bowl of mixed Greek olives and liberal sprinkles of sea salt, and our simple meal was complete. To this day, I'll never forget the way those olives tasted like the saltiness of the sea, and the cherry tomatoes like sunshine. I'm not sure if it was the fact that we were famished from our swim or the beautiful setting that made it so memorable, but there's no doubt that the freshness, seasonality, and simplicity of that meal will forever define the taste of Santorini in my mind.

Camille

These days, whether I'm recipe-testing for the blog or pulling together a quick meal for my family, I'm always on the hunt for ways to create the most bursting-with-flavor dishes while expending the least amount of time and effort. What I've discovered is that when I use fresh, seasonal ingredients, they shine brightest when I don't mess with them too much. I truly believe that any meal is only as good as the quality of what goes into it, so I try to start with fresh, mostly organic foods that look as close as possible to the way they grew in nature. There are so many messages out there about what *not* to eat, and after tons of reading and research, I've finally decided that a diet that includes a little bit of everything (yep, dairy and bread included) in its whole, natural state is what's best for me. That means I try not to eat things out of a package and avoid ingredient lists that have words too long to pronounce, and it also means that I get to be creative and come up with lots of different ways to prepare whatever produce is peak of season.

Of course, cooking with the seasons requires a little flexibility and a lot of open-mindedness. We subscribe to a weekly CSA (community-supported agriculture) box that we pick up every Saturday at the downtown farmers' market. The way it works is that members form a direct partnership with a farm—in my case, Johnson's Backyard Garden here in Austin—where they pay in advance for a share of its upcoming harvest. Everybody wins, since the farm is promised a consistent market, and the customer gets to take home a box brimming with beautiful, local, organic produce. It's become such a fun ritual to open up our box each week and start dreaming up meals to try out in the coming weeks to use up all of our produce. Of course, sometimes it means getting creative! Last weekend I got my first bunch of kohlrabi and had to do a bit of research before deciding to peel and chop it, then toss with olive oil, garlic, salt, and crushed red pepper flakes and roast in the oven with butternut squash. It was delicious and gave me great satisfaction to know that we'd taken a new flavor adventure with a vegetable that was plucked from the soil just a few miles from our home.

Taking the time on weekends to stock our fridge with high-quality, seasonal produce has totally changed our weeknight dinners. I'm always scouring websites and cookbooks for new, creative ways to use the abundant veggies in my CSA box—and as shown by the kohlrabi incident, I'm often challenged to cook with ingredients I might never have purchased otherwise! Even though we do eat all kinds of meat and fish at our house, I've noticed that we've just naturally been doing a lot more vegetarian dinners lately—comforting soups made with squash and sweet potatoes, salads brimming with roasted beets and avocados, quinoa salads with garbanzo beans and currants. We don't even miss the meat, and it's a great way to give our digestive systems a bit of a detoxifying break.

I used to think that when it came to farm-fresh eating, summer had all the fun, but it turns out that the fall and winter months are a beautiful time for fresh produce, too! For an autumn dinner party, I might kick things off with a salad of butter lettuce tossed with blue cheese, roasted pears, and toasted walnuts, then follow it up with butternut squash ravioli topped with brown butter and sage. Dessert would undoubtedly incorporate apples—maybe a crumble or crisp, crowned with a cinnamon-flecked streusel and a big scoop of vanilla bean ice cream.

Of course, sometimes you just might need some corn or peas in the dead of winter, and that's okay! Rather than buying totally out-of-season fresh produce, I prefer to buy frozen organic vegetables that were flash-frozen at their peak of season and keep them on hand throughout the winter. They'll taste great incorporated into recipes and retain almost all their nutrients when handled and frozen properly. This year I've even started experimenting with preserving. At the height of summer, my CSA box was brimming with more beets, okra, and cucumbers than we could ever eat, and pickling them yielded delicious results . . . and a pantry full of "summer" produce all year long!

If this way of thinking, cooking, and eating feels new and even a bit intimidating, don't be afraid to just dive in. There's no better time than the present to start feeding your body (and those of the people you love) beautiful, delicious, and healthful food, and it needn't be complex or difficult. The beauty of eating seasonal fruits and vegetables is that they taste their best with minimal preparation, so a drizzle of olive oil and a quick roast in the oven, paired with a piece of grilled fish or a pot of grains, is all you need for a gorgeous nutrition-packed meal. So head to the farmers' market this weekend and scoop up whatever looks interesting, talk to the farmers about which produce is at its very best, and then hop online and search for some yummy-sounding recipes to help inspire the prep. Make it fun by grabbing your significant other or inviting a girlfriend over to pop open a bottle of wine, turn on some relaxing music, and spend an evening in the kitchen celebrating delicious, good-for-you food together. I guarantee it'll become one of your favorite weekend rituals, and before you know it, you'll be cooking up great healthy, seasonal meals all week long.

8

FALL HORS D'OEUVRES

A great party starts with great appetizers. There's nothing like opening the door and greeting guests with a festive drink and a few beautiful little bites to whet their appetites and make them feel instantly at ease. But in order to keep myself sane in the kitchen, I stick to a couple rules when it comes to hors d'oeuvres. They either need to be quickly assembled from a few store-bought ingredients or, if made from scratch, I must be able to prepare them almost completely the night before. I talk more about my favorite simple appetizers on page 171, and here I'm sharing a few lovely little jewels that showcase fall ingredients at their finest.

Camille

Figs, Blue Cheese, and Pomegranate Seeds on Endive Leaves (page 44)

FIGS, BLUE CHEESE, AND POMEGRANATE SEEDS ON ENDIVE LEAVES

When I worked in catering, one of our most popular hors d'oeuvres was a luscious port wine–soaked cherry and blue cheese combo tucked into an endive leaf like a little boat. This is my autumnal version featuring figs and pomegranate for the most gorgeous color and a touch of exotic flavor. So many of my friends eat gluten-free diets these days, so this is a nice way to serve them a great blue cheese that doesn't require crackers or bread. You can make these up to an hour before the party, and the hearty leaves will hold up as they sit.

SERVES 8

5 fresh figs, each cut into 4 wedges

½ cup balsamic vinegar

2 heads Belgian endive, leaves separated (smallest leaves reserved for another use)

2 ounces blue cheese (Stilton, Cambozola, or any creamy blue cheese), at room temperature and crumbled

¼ cup Candied Pecans (see sidebar), finely chopped

¼ cup pomegranate seeds

¼ cup honey

Put the fig wedges in a small bowl and cover with the balsamic vinegar. Set aside and let macerate for at least 30 minutes (and up to overnight, in the fridge).

To assemble, lay out the endive leaves on a platter. Use a small spoon to scoop about ½ teaspoon of blue cheese into each leaf. Top each with a fig wedge, sprinkle with pecans and a couple pomegranate seeds, drizzle with honey, and serve.

CANDIED PECANS

½ cup pecan halves

½ cup sugar, plus more for sprinkling

Kosher salt

Preheat the oven to 400°F. In a small saucepan, combine the pecans, sugar, and 1 cup water; bring to a boil, and stir continuously until the sugar dissolves. Cook over medium heat for 5 minutes, stirring constantly. Use a slotted spoon to transfer the pecans to a baking sheet. Sprinkle with a bit of sugar and kosher salt, then bake for 8 minutes, or until the nuts are lightly caramelized. Let cool, then serve or store in an airtight container for up to 1 week.

(See photo on page 42.)

FENNEL AND CITRUS-MARINATED OLIVES

Olives are always a perfect choice for pairing with cocktails—their briny flavor is a delicious complement to everything from dry martinis to fizzy Champagne. While it's completely fine to just set out a bowl of olives with a few toothpicks and call it a night, why not make store-bought olives a little more party worthy by combining them with fennel seeds and citrus zest? All the prep work is done in advance, since they need to marinate overnight, and they can actually hang out in the fridge for a week. When it's party time, don't forget to set out a little bowl next to them for catching the pits!

MAKES 2 CUPS

2 cups unpitted olives (I like to use a mix of sizes, shapes, and colors)

Zest of 1 lemon, julienned

Zest of 1 lime, julienned

½ teaspoon fennel seeds

Crushed red pepper flakes

In a large mason jar, combine the olives with some of their juices, lemon zest, lime zest, fennel seeds, and a pinch of red pepper flakes (more or less, depending on how much heat you want). Toss to combine and then allow to marinate in the fridge overnight and up to 1 week.

GARLICKY EGGPLANT DIP

I love stumbling upon a recipe that tastes decadent but is actually quite healthy, and this eggplant-based dip certainly feels much richer than it actually is. Something magical happens when eggplant gets really charred on the outside—the inside becomes sweet, tender, and almost buttery, making it the perfect foundation for a dip that combines the Mediterranean flavors of garlic, tahini, and lemon juice. If you like your dip on the smoother side (or are serving guests who "think" they don't like eggplant), just throw all the ingredients in a blender and purée. Trust me: they won't know what hit 'em.

2 small eggplants, pricked all over with a fork

1 garlic clove, minced

2 tablespoons tahini (sesame paste)

2 teaspoons extra-virgin olive oil, plus more for drizzling

2 tablespoons fresh lemon juice

Kosher salt and freshly ground black pepper

Toasted pine nuts, for garnish (see sidebar)

Minced fresh parsley, for garnish

Preheat the broiler. Place the eggplants on a foil-lined baking sheet and broil 6 inches from the heat until charred all over, turning every 5 minutes (the entire process will take about 20 minutes). Set aside to cool and then remove the skin and add the flesh to a large bowl.

Add the garlic, tahini, oil, and lemon juice. Use a potato masher to mash the eggplant and combine all the ingredients. You want it well mixed but still chunky. Season to taste with salt and pepper and transfer to a serving bowl. Drizzle with olive oil and sprinkle the pine nuts and parsley over the top. Serve with raw vegetables and pita crisps.

HOW TO TOAST NUTS

Toasting nuts is a crucial step in many of my recipes—once you taste the depth of flavor and added crunch that a light toast gives pecans, walnuts, and pine nuts, you'll never want to go back to using raw nuts in a recipe again! Whether they'll be baked in a cake or tossed into a salad, here are a few simple steps to making sure that yours turn out perfectly.

Adjust an oven rack to the lower third of the oven and preheat the oven to 350°F. Spread the nuts in a single layer on a baking sheet and place it on the rack.

As a general rule of thumb, pine nuts and sliced almonds will be done in about 5 minutes, while pecans, walnuts, and hazelnuts will take 10 minutes or so. Since ovens heat differently, keep a close eye on them, and stir the nuts halfway through to ensure even cooking.

You'll know they're ready when you just begin to smell their nutty scent wafting from the oven; since toasting nuts releases their essential oils, they become incredibly fragrant. Just be sure to pull them out of the oven *right* when this happens, since an extra couple of minutes may result in blackened nuts with a too-charred flavor. It's happened to me far too many times!

After removing from the oven, transfer nuts to a clean plate to stop the cooking. Let cool completely.

"SINFUL" APPLE WEDGES

One of the best qualities of hors d'oeuvres is that they're only a couple of bites, and since I don't typically include a lot of bacon in my diet, these diminutive appetizers are the perfect way to satisfy my cravings. The apple caramelizes in the oven and becomes candylike against the salty, crisp bacon. These devilish little guys are some of my very favorite accompaniments to a glass of crisp Champagne—just be sure to make enough, since the temptation for just one more might be too great for your guests.

MAKES 24 WEDGES

1 large Granny Smith apple

8 slices thick-cut bacon

¼ cup pure maple syrup

20 baby arugula leaves

Coarse sea salt

Preheat the oven to 375˚F. Line a baking sheet with foil. On the stovetop, heat a cast-iron skillet to medium-high.

Halve and core the apple and then cut each half into 6 slices. Cut each slice in half. Use kitchen shears to slice bacon in half lengthwise and then halve again crosswise (each bacon slice will yield 4 pieces).

Wrap each piece of apple in a strip of bacon and place seam side down in the hot skillet. You should hear a sizzle when it hits. Use a spatula to lightly press each piece down so that the seams cook together. When the bacon is browned and almost crispy on the bottom, flip and brown the other side of the bacon, and then carefully transfer the skillet to the oven. Cook for 5 to 8 minutes, until the apples are tender, and then remove from the oven and brush each piece with a tiny bit of maple syrup.

Transfer to a serving platter, let cool for a minute or two, and then carefully stick a little arugula leaf between each apple and bacon slice. Sprinkle with a little salt and serve with toothpicks.

THYME POPOVERS WITH GINGER-PEAR BUTTER

I'll never forget going to lunch at the Zodiac Room at Neiman Marcus with my mom as a little girl. To my ten-year-old self, it was the ultimate in ladies-who-lunch propriety, and every detail about our meals there felt magical, from the models who paraded around the dining room to the endless assortment of tea sandwiches. But my favorite part was the baskets of steaming popovers slathered with strawberry butter that began every meal. Today I adore making fluffy popovers for the people I love, and this thyme-flecked version with ginger-pear butter is my updated-for-fall version. I make these in a mini-muffin pan for the perfect two-bite appetizer, but you could certainly use a popover pan to get even taller, more generously sized portions (triple the recipe to yield 8 larger popovers). The key to getting the puffiest popovers is high heat, so be sure to open and close the oven door as quickly as possible.

1 large egg

½ cup whole milk

½ cup all-purpose flour

¼ teaspoon salt

½ tablespoon unsalted butter, melted

Leaves from 4 fresh thyme sprigs

Vegetable oil, for the pan

Ginger-Pear Butter (see sidebar)

In a medium bowl, whisk the egg and milk until well combined and frothy. Sift in the flour and salt and then use a spatula to stir to just combined but still lumpy.

Slowly whisk in the butter. Continue whisking until the batter is completely smooth, about 30 seconds. Let the batter rest in the fridge for 1 hour.

Meanwhile, adjust the oven rack to the lowest position and preheat the oven to 450°F. Pour a drop of vegetable oil into each of 8 mini-muffin tins and swirl the pan to coat the bottom of each cup. Place the pan in the oven and let it heat for 30 minutes.

Pour the batter into a container with a spout, such as a measuring cup, and then remove the pan from the oven and shut the door. Working as quickly as possible, fill each of the 8 muffin cups almost to the top and return the pan to the oven.

Bake for 15 minutes. Reduce the heat to 350°F and bake another 5 to 8 minutes, until golden brown. To remove the popovers, invert the pan onto a cooling rack, carefully using a sharp knife to loosen any that might have stuck to the pan.

Serve immediately with ginger-pear butter.

GINGER-PEAR BUTTER

1 CUP

1 very ripe pear

1½ tablespoons pure maple syrup

8 tablespoons (1 stick) unsalted butter, at room temperature

½ teaspoon ground cinnamon

1 teaspoon freshly grated ginger

⅛ teaspoon kosher salt

Preheat the oven to 400°F and line a baking sheet with foil.

Peel, quarter, and core the pear. Place the pear quarters on the prepared baking sheet and brush the tops with maple syrup. Bake for 20 minutes, or until the pear is very tender. Set aside and let cool slightly and then mash until no large lumps remain.

In a medium bowl, combine the butter, mashed pear, cinnamon, ginger, and salt and stir until smooth. Cover and refrigerate for up to 1 week.

9

DEVELOPING A SIGNATURE STYLE

In a roundabout way, the world of fashion actually led to my career in parties and events. As a twenty-one-year-old journalism student, I dreamed of a career working in fashion magazines, covering designers' latest collections, and styling glamorous photo shoots around the world. When I scored my "dream" internship at a fashion public relations firm in New York City, I headed to Manhattan in pursuit of being the next Anna Wintour. I'll never forget that first day on the job: six hours organizing the shoe closet overflowing with mismatched pairs of last season's samples, hopping the subway to SoHo to pick up an iPod for one of my bosses' kid's birthday, and then hoofing it through Times Square in ninety-degree heat, weighed down with garment bags as I made my way to Condé Nast to drop off pieces for a photo shoot. *At least I'll finally get a peek inside the* Vogue *offices, right?* I thought (naively). Wrong. When I arrived, I was directed to the door of the alleyway loading dock where I was not-so-promptly greeted by a courier who grabbed the bags from my hand and shut the door. So much for glamour!

If you guessed that the rest of the summer proceeded in a similar manner, you were right. And while I'd never

Camille

knock the fashion industry as a whole—it's full of some of the most energetic and creative people I know!—I realized fairly quickly that it just wasn't for me. The upside is that during my time at the firm I ended up falling head over heels for the incredible events that my bosses dreamed up for our clients. Each party had its own unique set of challenges, requiring a fresh eye and loads of creativity, making the day-to-day incredibly exciting and never boring. I was hooked, and when I made the decision to move to Austin soon after, I quickly scored a job as an event planner for a catering company—and the rest is history.

Although I ultimately chose a different career, I still really love fashion and the way the perfect outfit can express a woman's individuality and fill her with confidence. It's all about discovering your personal style, sussing out which of those signature pieces and colors make you feel the most you. Knowing your style becomes especially important when entertaining, since you need to be able to throw on something that's beautiful and fits your body well and then go host a party without giving your outfit another thought. To those who might think spending a significant amount of time talking about fashion is vain, I'd say that defining your style and discovering your best look actually allows you to be more focused on others. When you feel comfortable with your appearance (instead of fussing with a hemline or second-guessing your outfit choice), you're free to greet your guests and lavish them with all your focused attention—the mark of a great hostess.

Knowing your style doesn't require an unlimited budget or staying on top of what designers are sending down runways each season. Think about the outfits that when you're wearing them make you feel like the very best version of yourself. Is it a short cocktail dress or a long, flowing caftan? A classic white button-down or a trend-of-the-moment look decked out with loads of jewelry? Of course, the type of party you're hosting will dictate to some degree how dressy or casual you are, but within these general boundaries there's a lot of wiggle room to wear something that's a reflection of you. If you're not really sure what your personal style is, spend some time taking inventory of your closet: make a list of the pieces you feel great in, that you return to over and over. My list includes short shift dresses, striped tops, silk button-downs, very dark jeans, and wedge espadrilles. If I'm wearing any version of these, I usually feel very "me," which translates into confidence. It can also be helpful to put your style into words, which can help filter out the pieces that aren't the best fit. Is your look tailored or trendy, feminine or androgynous, ladylike or edgy? Most people are a mix; for example, as I've mentioned, I define my style as classic and understated with a dash of bohemian.

Once you know your style, it's well worth it to do a little **advance outfit planning** before hosting any type of get-together. Ten minutes before the party is *not* the time to be staring at your closet trying to pull an outfit together. Take time a week before an event to choose an outfit that you know you'll feel great in, and (this part is crucial), *try it on.* I can't count the number of times I've thrown on a dress before a party only to realize that I didn't have quite the right undergarments to go with it, or the accessories I'd envisioned wearing didn't quite "work" with the overall look, or I hadn't worn it in a while and the fit was off. Try everything on (including shoes), do a few turns in front of a full-length mirror, and get ready to work that party like nobody's business.

As unglamorous as it may sound, don't forget that **comfort is key** when hosting, or even attending, a party. It doesn't matter how fierce those four-inch heels make your legs look: if you're wobbling around or walking with a temporary limp, they aren't worth it. (I once heard it said that more important than a pair of shoes is knowing how to walk in them gracefully. So true!) Since the whole point of a party is to have fun and celebrate, any part of your outfit that gets in the way of that should be banned as far as I'm concerned. And since you're trying everything on in advance, it's the perfect time to walk around and make sure you're not pulling at your hem, repeatedly

hiding your bra strap, adjusting your neckline, or feeling the need to suck in your stomach. You'll be way too busy drinking wine and laughing with friends to worry about any of those annoyances!

When you've planned an outfit that reflects your signature style and that you'll be able to celebrate comfortably in, it's time to add **one festive element**. It's a party, after all! For me, this often looks like one show-stopping accessory that elevates a look without appearing to try too hard: a trend-of-the-moment hat, a bright pair of shoes, a chunky menswear watch, or a statement necklace will jazz up a cocktail dress I may have worn loads of times before. I usually splurge on one or two really special accessories every season— that way, I can add a punch of newness to last year's dress and feel like a million bucks. And for gals like me who have a more classic style, accessories are the perfect way to get a little adventurous and dip your toe into the waters of a new trend.

So what are you waiting for? Go ahead, set off on a style identity quest, and don't forget to have fun along the way. Carve out your own distinct look, and throw out those dated dress codes and fashion rules that are better left ignored. Embracing your individuality and feeling beautiful just as you are is the true essence of chic. And a swipe of vibrant lipstick has also never let me down.

10

PICNIC AT THE FARM

>>>>>>>>> A BIRTHDAY PARTY <<<<<<<<<

When I was a kid, I'd start planning my birthday party *months* in advance. After all, there was lots to be done!: put in a birthday cake order with the chef (my mom), design custom invitations (hand-drawn with colored pencils by *moi*), and come up with the perfect, party-worthy location (swimming pools and skating rinks were always popular picks). Now that I have a daughter of my own, I'm having just as much fun creating a concept and putting together a handful of details to make birthday parties magical for the kids and grown-ups alike.

To welcome the cooler weather, I invited a few kids and their moms to join us at a local farm to celebrate our friend Parker's fourth birthday and enjoy an autumn lunch under the big oak tree. We packed picnic baskets with baguette sandwiches, tabbouleh salad, and pickled veggies in mason jars, as well as cozy blankets that would let us spread out and give the little ones room to play. The chicken coop and vegetable patches provided built-in entertainment, and an old farm table became a festive spot for birthday cake and rowdy games of Pin the Tail on the Piglet. If only turning another year older could *always* be such fun!

Camille

We packed picnic baskets with baguette sandwiches, tabbouleh salad, and pickled veggies in mason jars, as well as cozy blankets that would let us spread out and give the little ones room to play.

The
MENU

PICNIC AT THE FARM

When packing a picnic, the two main things to keep in mind are the *temperature* and the *durability* of the food. Room-temperature items are great, since it means not having to pack everything on ice or heat it up on-site. You also want items that will hold up well and won't become soggy. Crusty breads like baguettes are great sandwich choices, since they don't absorb a lot of moisture, and when it comes to salads, crunchy vegetables like radishes, carrots, and cucumbers won't go limp. This menu is totally kid-friendly but "gourmet" enough that the adults still feel treated to a delicious feast.

TO DRINK	PACKED FOR A PICNIC	FOR THE BIRTHDAY CELEBRATION
APPLE-GINGER JUICE (FOR THE KIDS), PAGE 70	TURKEY, APPLE, AND BRIE SANDWICHES, PAGE 71	APPLE CAKE WITH CARAMEL GLAZE, PAGE 76
SPIKED PEAR-THYME SPARKLERS (FOR THE MOMS), PAGE 70	CHEDDAR, FIG, AND CARAMELIZED ONION SANDWICHES, PAGE 72	JUMBO FARM "ANIMAL CRACKER" COOKIES
	ISRAELI COUSCOUS TABBOULEH, PAGE 75	
	PICKLED VEGETABLES, FRESH APPLES, AND BERRIES FOR SNACKING	

GET THE LOOK

One of the best parts about a beautiful outdoor location is that the decor is practically done for you! I love the rustic simplicity of Springdale Farm, and the only adornment needed is some big cozy blankets to spread out on the grass, a few wooden crates that do double duty as food carriers and impromptu seating, a bunch of balloons, and a few handmade garlands to string over an old wooden door. Inspired by autumn apple orchards, I stuck with a classic color palette of red, denim, burlap, and slate that looked perfectly in keeping with our rustic surroundings.

The cake always makes a festive focal point for any birthday celebration, so I topped a vintage farm table with colorful oilcloth (whimsical and, more important, stain resistant!) and placed the cake on a vintage stand that added height and drama. The market chalkboard became our birthday sign, and a few handmade paper party hats marked each place at the table. A picnic is a great opportunity to keep it simple and work with what you've got, so start by looking at what's already at your location. At a farm, hay bales make perfect seating, and produce plucked from the field is an ideal centerpiece. When you open up your eyes to what's all around, you just might discover that there's an instant party practically waiting to happen!

HORSING AROUND

A farm provides tons of built-in entertainment, since there's nothing kids would rather do than watch the chickens, pet the animals, and explore the endless rows of vegetable crops. And with small children like Phoebe, it's a fun learning opportunity to teach them about the different animals and let them see where the fruits and vegetables they regularly eat actually come from!

To add a dose of extra excitement, I put a new twist on an old-fashioned game with a handmade Pin the Tail on the Piglet board. Hang it on a fence or the side of a building, blindfold the kids, and let them try their hand at attaching the piglet's "tail," made from curly pipe cleaners attached to circles cut from strong tape. Other retro games that are sure to be a hit? Horseshoes, bocce ball, croquet, badminton—even just a game of catch will keep boredom at bay.

TAKING IT TO GO

Though packing a picnic is a spontaneous pleasure that should be seized upon at the first signs of beautiful weather, I do take a few steps to make sure people are comfortable and food isn't soggy.

1 | When scouting your location, choose a picnic spot with care: dry, flat ground under the shade of a tree is perfect. Pack a few blankets to scatter on the grass, and consider packing food in wooden crates or sturdy boxes that can be flipped over and used as tabletops and seating.

2 | Bring a big cutting board or two that can be used as a flat, steady surface for serving food and drinks. This will keep them from tipping over on the grass.

3 | If some of your food items need to be served cold, pack them in a cooler with ice and separate them from room-temperature items. Decant beverages into glass bottles with lids, and bring mason jars or disposable cups for sipping.

4 | Forgo the plastic stuff and bring disposable bamboo flatware for an easy and effortless touch. Instead of plates, I packed salad in individual jars with lids that would prevent spills and wrapped sandwiches in parchment paper that could be tossed when the meal was over.

5 | Don't forget the trash bags, paper towels, and a few moist towelettes for cleaning everything (and everyone) up when your picnic is done!

When scouting your location, choose a picnic spot with care: dry, flat ground under the shade of a tree is perfect. Pack a few blankets to scatter on the grass.

QUEEN FOR A DAY

The most memorable thing about birthdays is that magical feeling of being showered with adoration from everyone you love. Whether the guest of honor is young or, well, trying to lose count of exactly *which* birthday this is, here are a few ways to make them feel like a million bucks.

FACE TIME.

For Adam's fortieth birthday, I printed out childhood photos of him and plastered them all over the party, from the cocktail stir sticks to the bottoms of hors d'oeuvre trays. Everyone got a kick out of seeing little baby Adam peeking out at them in unlikely places. What a fun way to make sure no one forgets whose party it is!

LIFE STORY.

Create an invitation that maps out the guest of honor's life, with a timeline containing all the major milestones (first job, first car, personal and professional achievements). Make it a mix of serious moments (meeting their spouse) with more lighthearted ones (buying their first pair of skinny jeans).

PARTY PLAYLIST.

If the birthday girl or guy loves to reminisce about an earlier decade, create a playlist that features all the hits from that era. There's nothing a child of the seventies would love more than a birthday dinner serenaded by the Bee Gees' greatest hits.

COMPLIMENTS OF THE CHEF.

My mom is an incredible baker, and our entire family looks forward to putting in their birthday cake order a couple weeks before the big day. The tradition dictates that they can request *anything* they want, no matter how untraditional! I've ordered everything from homemade peach ice cream to a big trifle bowl of banana pudding. Just 'cause it's not cake doesn't mean you can't put a candle in it!

PHOTO OP.

When you send out invitations, ask everyone to mail in their favorite (preferably funny) photos of the guest of honor through the years. At the party, have a slideshow of the photos rolling to provide endless entertainment throughout the evening. And the perfect birthday gift? Have a photo album printed for the birthday boy or girl containing all the photos, with captions written by the guests.

RAISE A GLASS.

Especially for milestone birthdays, allowing time for a few toasts gives guests a chance to express what the guest of honor has meant in their life . . . or at least share some funny story that will crack everyone up! Whether or not you're a fan of public displays, here are a few dos and don'ts to keep in mind for toasting success.

DO *keep it short and snappy. Two to five minutes, max, and limit your anecdotes to one great one.*

DO *prepare in advance, but* **DON'T** *read word for word off a piece of paper unless you want the audience to think you Googled your speech.*

DO *read a few lines from a great poem or an inspiring quote if you can't think of quite what to say. Can't go wrong!*

DO *crack a joke, but keep it clean. And* **DON'T** *tell any stories that will truly embarrass the guest of honor. If you're concerned that their feelings might be hurt by that funny story, play it safe and* **DON'T** *tell it.*

DO *wrap it up by raising your glass and closing with a celebratory "To [insert guest of honor's name here]."*

As a nod to one of autumn's quintessential activities, I filled a wooden bucket with apples for each child to take home. They served as healthy snacks.

To: lulu
love, parker

To: phoebe
love, parker

THE FAVORS

As a nod to one of autumn's quintessential activities, I filled a wooden bucket with apples for each child to take home. They served as healthy snacks during the party, and afterward kids will find all kinds of uses for the classic buckets! Phoebe uses hers to collect acorns in our driveway, and it just might become a makeshift trick-or-treat bucket once October 31 rolls around. The buckets can be found at a craft or hardware store—just tie a label with each child's name onto the handle and fill with apples, pears, or even miniature pumpkins and winter squash.

bottoms up!

I packed glass bottles of apple-ginger juice for kids and spiked pear-thyme sparklers for the moms. Both are best prepared the day before, so the morning of the picnic, all you have to do is pack them up in a cooler. Don't forget the straws!

APPLE-GINGER JUICE

SERVES 6 TO 8

Mix 2 quarts high-quality apple juice with a 4-inch piece of peeled fresh ginger that has been cut into 4 pieces. Allow to chill in the fridge overnight so the flavors really meld. The morning of the picnic, strain out the ginger pieces and use a funnel to decant the juice into individual glass bottles.

SOURCES

Location: SpringdaleFarm
Food styling: Ann Lowe
Invitations & paper goods: Antiquaria
Props: Loot Vintage Rentals
Table linens: Serena & Lily
Dinnerware & glassware: Anthropologie

SPIKED PEAR-THYME SPARKLERS

SERVES 6 TO 8

The morning before the picnic, make a thyme simple syrup by heating 1 cup sugar, 1 cup water, and 10 fresh thyme sprigs over medium-high heat. Bring to a boil and stir for a minute until the sugar has dissolved. Refrigerate until chilled and then discard the thyme.

Combine 3 cups pear-infused vodka, 1 cup apple juice, 1 thinly sliced pear, and 1 cup thyme simple syrup and refrigerate for at least 2 hours or overnight to allow the flavors to meld. The morning of the picnic, decant into bottles to transport. At the picnic, fill glasses two-thirds full with the mixture, top off with chilled sparkling water, and garnish with thyme sprigs.

TURKEY, APPLE, AND BRIE SANDWICHES

What could be better than the classic cheese board combination of crisp apple slices and creamy Brie? How about a sandwich inspired by that duo, topped with turkey and spread with indulgent apple butter for the perfect autumnal lunch? This sandwich is great served at room temperature for a picnic, but if you decide to make it on a cozy night indoors, fire up the griddle and make it into the best panini you'll ever taste.

MAKES 8 SANDWICHES

16 slices rye bread

3 tablespoons good-quality store-bought apple butter

8 ounces thinly sliced turkey breast

6 ounces creamy Brie, sliced into 16 pieces

2 Granny Smith apples, cored and thinly sliced

On half of the bread slices, spread a teaspoon of apple butter. Evenly divide the turkey, Brie, and apple slices onto each slice and then top with the remaining bread slices. Use a serrated knife to cut each sandwich diagonally.

CHEDDAR, FIG, AND CARAMELIZED ONION SANDWICHES

This sandwich is a total crowd-pleaser, with figs and caramelized onions that are as sweet as candy, melding with the saltiness of really good sharp Cheddar. If you don't like the chewiness of a baguette, this would be great on slices of toasted multigrain or ciabatta, too. Caramelize the onions the night before the picnic, and in the morning all that's left to do is assemble the sandwiches and wrap them in parchment paper for transport.

SERVES 8

2 tablespoons butter

2 sweet onions, sliced

2 teaspoons sugar

1 French baguette, split horizontally

16 thin slices sharp Cheddar

8 fresh Black Mission figs, trimmed and cut lengthwise into ¼-inch-thick slices

A few handfuls of baby arugula leaves

Coarse sea salt

Melt the butter in a large skillet over medium heat. Add the onions and sauté until just tender, about 6 minutes. Reduce the heat to medium-low and cook until the onions are golden, stirring often, about 20 minutes. Sprinkle the sugar over the onions and sauté 20 more minutes, until the onions are golden brown, reduced, and very sweet. If the pan gets dry, add a little water. (The onions shouldn't burn at all.) Set aside to cool. (This can be done a day in advance and kept in the refrigerator.)

Spread the caramelized onions in an even layer on the bottom half of the baguette. Top with the Cheddar, fig slices, baby arugula, and a sprinkle of sea salt. Top with the other baguette half, then use a serrated knife to cut the baguette into 8 equal sandwiches.

ISRAELI COUSCOUS TABBOULEH

I'm a huge fan of tabbouleh, the classic Middle Eastern salad that's typically made from bulgur, tomatoes, cucumbers, and loads of herbs. For this version, I substituted Israeli couscous, a satisfyingly chewy pearl-shaped pasta that's always a hit with kids, and amped up the fall flavors with radishes and an apple. Pack into mason jars for an easily totable side that's as perfect for school lunch boxes as for picnic baskets.

SERVES 8 AS A SIDE

3 tablespoons olive oil

1 garlic clove, minced

1 cup Israeli couscous

1¼ cups chicken broth

Zest and juice of 1 lemon

Kosher salt and freshly ground black pepper

¼ cup chopped fresh flat-leaf parsley

⅓ cup chopped fresh mint

¼ cup chopped green onions

6 radishes, cleaned, stems removed, and chopped

1 seedless cucumber, peeled and chopped

½ green apple, cored and chopped

Squeeze of honey

In a medium saucepan, heat 1 tablespoon of the oil and sauté the minced garlic for about 30 seconds, until just barely golden. Add the couscous and cook, stirring, about 3 minutes to get it a bit toasty. Add the broth and bring to a boil. Cover and cook over low heat until the couscous is tender and the liquid is absorbed, about 10 minutes.

In a large bowl, whisk together the lemon zest and juice and 1 tablespoon of the oil. Season with salt and pepper and stir in the couscous. Refrigerate until it reaches room temperature, about 1 hour.

Up to an hour before serving, add the parsley, mint, green onions, radishes, cucumber, and apple and toss well. Season with more salt and pepper, drizzle the remaining tablespoon of olive oil and the honey over the top, toss, and serve.

APPLE CAKE WITH CARAMEL GLAZE

If ever there was a "taste" of autumn, this Bundt cake is it. The simple recipe combines lots of my favorite things (cinnamon, apples, carrots, and ginger!) into one impressive-looking and addictively delicious spice cake. And I love that all the ingredients get dumped into one bowl! This recipe calls for a 15-cup capacity Bundt pan, which is quite large. If your pan is smaller, simply pour the excess batter into muffin cups and reduce the cooking time for scrumptious apple-caramel cupcakes.

CAKE

½ cup raisins

½ cup dark rum

2½ cups all-purpose flour

1½ teaspoons baking powder

¾ teaspoon baking soda

1 teaspoon ground allspice

1½ teaspoons ground cinnamon

1 teaspoon freshly grated nutmeg

¼ teaspoon ground cloves

1 teaspoon kosher salt

1½ cups (firmly packed) light brown sugar, sifted

1½ cups granulated sugar

¾ pound (3 sticks) unsalted butter, softened

4 large eggs

1 large egg yolk

2 teaspoons pure vanilla extract

3 Granny Smith or Gala apples, peeled, cored, and diced

1 cup grated carrot

1 cup toasted walnuts, coarsely chopped (see page 47)

¼ cup finely chopped crystallized ginger

CARAMEL GLAZE

6 tablespoons (¾ stick) butter, chopped

¾ cup (packed) light brown sugar

½ cup heavy cream

½ teaspoon kosher salt

1½ cups confectioners' sugar

Position a rack in the middle of the oven and preheat it to 350°F. Butter and flour a 15-cup-capacity Bundt pan and set aside.

Put the raisins in a small bowl. Add the rum and set aside.

Sift the flour, baking powder, baking soda, allspice, cinnamon, nutmeg, and cloves into the bowl of an electric mixer. Add the salt, sugars, butter, eggs, egg yolk, and vanilla to the bowl. Mix on medium-high speed for 2 minutes, until light and fluffy, scraping the sides and beater with a spatula as needed.

Drain the raisins (discarding the rum) and add them to the batter with the apples, carrot, walnuts, and ginger. Stir on the lowest setting until combined and then use a spatula to scrape the bottom of the bowl, ensuring that everything is evenly distributed.

Pour the batter into the prepared pan and smooth the top. Bake for 1 hour and 15 minutes, or until a wooden skewer inserted into the center of the cake comes out clean and the sides start to pull away from the pan. Cool the cake in the pan for 15 minutes. Use a sharp knife to gently separate the cake from the sides of the pan. Invert the cake onto a cooling rack on a parchment-lined baking sheet and unmold. Let cool completely.

To make the glaze, in a medium saucepan, combine the butter, brown sugar, cream, and salt and bring to a boil, stirring continuously. Boil for 1 to 1½ minutes, or until the caramel is thickened slightly and light in color.

Remove from the heat and allow to cool for a minute and then whisk in the confectioners' sugar, a little at a time. Use only as much confectioners' sugar as you need to achieve a thick but easy-to-pour consistency. Slowly pour the glaze over the cooled cake, allowing it to drip down both sides. Once the glaze has set, transfer the cake to a platter or cake stand, then slice and serve. The cake will keep covered at room temperature for up to 3 days.

HOW TO MAKE YOUR INVITATION STAND OUT

Emma and Bailey of Antiquaria Design Studio

DESIGN.

The invitation is the first glimpse of your party that guests will see, so it's a great way to set the tone. Vivid colors, bold graphics, and modern patterns give a fun and playful vibe, whereas muted, neutral colors, simple graphics, clean lines, and classic patterns imply a more formal event.

COLOR.

Color can be used in ways other than just the printed invitation. A patterned envelope liner or a ribbon tied around the invitation can add brilliant shots of color while not breaking the bank, and tying in the color palette that will be used at the actual party gives guests a sense of what's to come.

ADDRESSING.

As calligraphers, of course, we love a beautifully hand-addressed envelope — there's nothing quite like receiving one in your mailbox to brighten your day! Hiring a calligrapher is a great option if your budget allows, but enlisting the help of a friend or family member with pretty handwriting to address envelopes can achieve a similar effect. Make sure to use a pen that is the same color as your return address for cohesion. For a digital option, check out online sources that offer calligraphy printing right onto the envelope or "icing" (a sticker band that wraps around the front and back of your envelope). Just don't use those office-standard white computer-generated labels, please!

POSTAGE.

Most people think of postage as simply the means to getting an invitation from point A to B, but a well-considered stamp goes a long way in making your envelope look "designed." We often try to find a stamp with colors or themes that complement the invitation and envelope. USPS.com offers a full assortment of what's currently available. Sometimes we even go so far as to seek out vintage postage to add a special flair. If you go this route, remember to buy *unused* postage. Champion Stamp Co. and eBay are great resources for vintage stamps. (By the way, there are services out there that will print custom postage with an image of your choosing, but they typically come with a big bar code that can overpower your design. In our opinion, it's not worth the extra cost.)

SENDING INVITATIONS.

Hand-canceling your envelopes at the post office will ensure that invitations arrive without those ugly bar codes printed on them. Insider tip: The US Postal Service charges extra to do this, but if you ask nicely, they'll usually let you do it yourself for no additional cost. And always remember to mail one to yourself! It's good to know when others might be receiving them, and it makes for a fun keepsake (we usually recommend having one postmarked and one un-postmarked invitation for photography purposes).

11

A THANKSGIVING FEAST

Since we don't have loads of relatives coming in town for Thanksgiving this year, I'll be hosting a cozy dinner in front of the fire for just our parents and a couple of close friends. I already talked about my love for Thanksgiving tradition (despite my rocky start as the host!) on page 12, and when each November rolls around, I start dreaming up ideas for putting a fresh twist on the big meal—honoring tradition while charming my guests with a few unexpected touches.

This year's surprises start with the menu: instead of roasting a whole turkey as I've done in the past, I'm stuffing and roasting a turkey breast—not only does it make for a beautiful presentation, it's also much easier to "get right" and end up

with a moist, flavorful piece of turkey with every bite. I'm also going to mix up the routine by setting up the Thanksgiving table in an unexpected location: I'm relocating our long wood dining table to a cozy spot in front of the living room fireplace. It'll undoubtedly change the entire dynamic of the meal, transforming it into a special occasion. Plus, nothing creates a magical glow like being surrounded by flickering candles and the warmth of firelight.

We have so much to be thankful for, and a quiet Thanksgiving surrounded by family, friends, and a bountiful feast will be the perfect way to count our blessings from the past year as we savor the present deliciously.

Camille

The MENU

A THANKSGIVING FEAST

APPETIZER

PEARS, CAMBOZOLA CHEESE, HONEYCOMB, AND FRUIT-STUDDED CRACKERS

Wine pairing: Chenin Blanc, Vouvray Demi-Sec, Loire Valley, France

ON THE BUFFET

BRUSSELS SPROUT AND APPLE SALAD WITH CIDER VINAIGRETTE, PAGE 92

BOURBON AND BROWN SUGAR WHIPPED SWEET POTATOES, PAGE 93

SAUSAGE, CHERRY, AND SAGE-STUFFED TURKEY BREAST, PAGE 94

APRICOT AND CRANBERRY CHUTNEY, PAGE 96

PARKER HOUSE ROLLS WITH THYME AND SEA SALT

Wine pairing: Gamay, Beaujolais-Morgon, Burgundy, France

FOR DESSERT

MAPLE PECAN TART, PAGE 97

Wine pairing: Bual Madeira, Portugal

Brussels Sprout and Apple Salad with Cider Vinaigrette (page 92)

GET THE LOOK

For this table design, I chose a palette of indigo, earthy wood, organic greens, and white in lieu of the more expected autumnal oranges and browns and chose table linens, dishes, serving pieces, and flowers that fit into those color families. Sticking within a limited palette is the quickest way to make a major visual impact while keeping the details simple!

A beautiful indigo runner and napkins in raw linen anchor each place setting and allow the beauty of a natural wood table to be revealed. Simple white plates make a statement in unexpected shapes without distracting from the colorful food that's the real star of the show.

In the fall, I love to think beyond flowers and forage for beautiful leaves and interesting berries or acorns to incorporate into a centerpiece. Pomegranates, winter squash, and pears also make unexpected additions to the table and are a modern spin on the iconic image of an abundant cornucopia. And since Thanksgiving is all about tradition, I love to honor the past by incorporating family heirlooms or treasured antiques on the table. I added a metallic glint with my mom's vintage brass candlesticks, which added a bit of polish to the otherwise natural centerpiece. And, of course, if there are family recipes that recall holidays past, let them find a place on your table amid newer menu items.

FALLING LEAVES

I recruited my friend Elizabeth of the floral studio the Nouveau Romantics to create the floral elements for this Thanksgiving feast, and she took her inspiration from the autumnal hues of turning leaves.

The buffet gets dressed up with a gorgeous copper pitcher full of greens, including bush ivy, oak leaves, grasses, and wheat. When creating a single-hued arrangement, you'll get the most impact by limiting the varieties to three or four types. The key is to use different tones of a single shade; in this case, greens ranging from forest to chartreuse.

We adorned the mantel with a lush oak-leaf garland. After an afternoon spent foraging for branches, Liz cut small segments from each one and attached them together using sturdy floral wire. The large oak leaves ensured that this one had plenty of volume.

The dining table centerpieces echo the buffet arrangement by incorporating some of the same types of greenery (bush ivy and wheat) but are made much more dramatic with the addition of flowers in saturated tones. Use large, statement-making pieces (like these artichokes and dahlias) for a beautiful focal point and to take up space, and then balance their drama by tucking in smaller, fine-textured flowers like ranunculus and astrantia. The finishing touch? Antique brass candlesticks of all different heights run down the center of the table to add flickering light and vintage charm.

COUNT YOUR BLESSINGS

Giving guests a chance to share what they're most thankful for is a great way to reflect, so why not turn those thoughts into tangible keepsakes by writing them down? During dessert, pass handmade cards around the table and ask everyone to write their name on one side and, on the other, jot down what they're grateful for this year. Once everyone's read their answers aloud, pack all the cards into a large envelope and write the date on the front. Do this every Thanksgiving to log your family's growth and follow everyone's personal journeys over the years.

MAKING THE CARDS

1 | *Begin with a 4.25 × 5.5-inch note card in the color of your choice—I chose indigo to coordinate with the vibrant runner on my table. Use scissors or a paper cutter to cut two card stock kraft paper rectangles: one 3.25 × 4.5 inches and the other 2 × 4.5 inches.*

2 | *Spread a glue stick onto one side of the larger rectangle and then adhere it directly to the center of the colored note card. Flip the note card over and adhere the smaller rectangle to the center.*

3 | *On the side with the larger piece of kraft paper, stamp a seasonal detail (like a pinecone, pumpkin, or turkey) in black ink onto the center of the card. Then use a stamp with a border design (such as a scroll or rectangle) above the seasonal image to create a space in which guests can fill in their name. Repeat until you have a card for each guest.*

MAKING THE ENVELOPES

1 | *Use an envelope that's at least 5.25 × 7.25 inches in a color that works with your decor. Create the decorative lining by laying an extra envelope on a flat surface with the opening faceup.*

2 | *Carefully pull on the adhesive to pull apart the folded-in flaps completely so that the inside of the envelope is exposed. Cut off the bottom and side flaps so that only the center of the envelope and top flap remain—this will be your liner template.*

3 | *Trace the liner template onto your favorite festive wrapping paper and cut out to create your decorative liner.*

4 | *Last, cut ½ inch off the bottom of the wrapping paper liner and then slide and glue into a new colored envelope.*

AN ABUNDANT BUFFET

   Although I love a family-style meal where big platters are passed around the table and shared, Thanksgiving is a day when I usually set up a buffet near the dining table. When a menu calls for more than three items, it's nice to move everything off the table so that it doesn't get too crowded. Plus, setting up a buffet lets everyone fill their plates with as much as they want of the items they love most . . . and of course, help themselves to the inevitable seconds! Here are a few keys to a great buffet setup:

1 | *Balancing a plate, napkin, and utensils while serving yourself can be a juggling act. To simplify the process, I like to preset all the napkins and silverware on the table so that guests have everything they need when they sit down. If you're hosting a larger gathering with more informal seating, place the plates at the beginning and the silverware and napkins at the end of the buffet to streamline the flow.*

2 | *Include a couple of menu items that can be served at room temperature so that you're not scrambling to get every single item out on the buffet at once. (I prefer not to use chafing dishes on a buffet at home, since they can be a bit of an eyesore.) For this menu, the appetizer can sit out unattended for a couple of hours during cocktails. And since the Brussels sprout salad and apricot and cranberry chutney are delicious at room temperature, set those out first while you slice the turkey and keep the sweet potatoes warm in the oven.*

3 | *Buffets look best with some variety in height. Use cake stands, tiered trays, or tall vases to add dimension to the display. To add interest to a collection of low serving pieces, try using stacked books, vintage crates, or overturned buckets as impromptu levels.*

VILMA'S TIPS ON THE PERFECT THANKSGIVING WINE

Vilma Mazaite of laV restaurant and wine bar in Austin

1. WHEN THERE'S LOTS OF VARIETY, GO LIGHT.

The challenge when pairing wine for a big meal like Thanksgiving is the wide variety of dishes and flavors that you'll load your plate with. For that reason, I suggest choosing a light wine that will go with a variety of foods. Great examples are many Pinot Noirs or Sauvignon Blancs. These varietals normally go better with a wider range of dishes.

2. FOR WHITES, GO UNOAKED.

I typically choose unoaked whites for the Thanksgiving meal. Since the dishes tend to be heavier and even slightly sweet (think cranberry sauce), I love a white wine with a little bit more sweetness and great acidity for balance, like a Riesling or Chenin Blanc. They help to mask the heaviness of those mashed potatoes so you can eat a little more without feeling overly full. It may be a dangerous strategy, but Thanksgiving dinner is only once a year; now's the time to go for it!

3. WHEN IN DOUBT, CHOOSE BUBBLES.

Sparkling wine makes any day a celebration, and it will certainly elevate the Thanksgiving meal—not to mention the fact that it has a magical effect on digestion. Choose rosé or vintage Champagne that has a little bit more body, and you can savor that glass throughout the entire dinner.

TURKEY-DAY TIMELINE

There's only one way to ensure a stress-free and seamless Thanksgiving: detailed, down-to-the-minute planning. Create a timeline for the twenty-four hours before mealtime, listing exactly when all menu items should be prepared, then put that list on the refrigerator door and follow it to the letter. We worked toward four o'clock in the afternoon as our turkey time this year, so if you plan to eat earlier or later, adjust your timeline accordingly. Here's what mine looked like this year:

DAY BEFORE THANKSGIVING.

Make the chutney and store it in an airtight container in the fridge. Set the table, arrange the flowers, and place serving pieces where they'll go on the buffet.

NIGHT BEFORE.

Prep the powder room, making sure the trash is empty, the soap is full, hand towels and toilet paper are well stocked, and there's a vase of flowers or a great-smelling candle next to the sink.

THANKSGIVING MORNING.

Completely prep the Brussels sprouts and apples, doing everything except the last step of tossing them in the dressing. Allow to cool and then refrigerate the salad in a covered dish or a couple of gallon-size freezer bags, storing the vinaigrette in a separate container.

FOUR HOURS BEFORE.

Prepare the stuffing and set it aside to cool. Preheat the oven. Chill the white wine.

THREE HOURS BEFORE.

Roll the turkey up with the stuffing and start roasting it.

TWO HOURS BEFORE.

Place the foil-wrapped sweet potatoes in the oven. Pop open a good bottle of sparkling wine to sip while you finish cooking—it's the holidays, after all! Fill a pitcher with filtered water and lemon slices and place in the fridge to get really cold.

THE BEATS

I played a throwback mix of songs that referenced gratitude, sure to be a hit among all ages. A sampling from my list:

Ray Davies, "Thanksgiving Day"
Simon & Garfunkel, "Leaves That Are Green"
The Beatles, "Thank You Girl"
The Byrds, "Turn! Turn! Turn!"
Jay & the Techniques, "Apples Peaches Pumpkin Pie"
Neil Diamond, "Thank the Lord for the Night Time"
Vince Guaraldi Trio, "Thanksgiving Theme"
Bob Marley, "Thank You Lord"

ONE HOUR BEFORE.

Arrange the cheese plate and set it out—it'll be ready and waiting for any early arrivals, and the cheese tastes better when it's come to room temperature. Remove the Brussels sprouts from the fridge and spread them on a foil-lined baking sheet.

THIRTY MINUTES BEFORE.

Pop the red wine in the fridge to chill slightly. Mash the roasted sweet potatoes with the other ingredients and arrange in a serving dish. Keep warm in the oven. Check the turkey for doneness—when it registers 150°F on a meat thermometer, cover with foil and allow to rest until ready to carve. While the turkey rests, reheat the Brussels sprouts in the oven and then toss in a serving bowl with the vinaigrette.

FIFTEEN MINUTES BEFORE.

If you have early-arriving guests, don't hesitate to give them simple tasks like opening the wine and slicing lemons for the water. Giving them a specific activity will actually put everyone at ease, but be sure to offer them a glass of wine to enjoy while they work!

TURKEY TIME!

Place everything in its designated spot on the buffet, call your guests to help themselves, then kick back and enjoy the feast.

SOURCES

Food styling: Ann Lowe
Floral design: The Nouveau Romantics
Calligraphy: Antiquaria
Table linens: Serena & Lily
Dinnerware & glassware: Anthropologie

BRUSSELS SPROUT AND APPLE SALAD WITH CIDER VINAIGRETTE

SERVES 8

SALAD

1 cup golden raisins

2 pounds Brussels sprouts, trimmed and halved (quartered if very large)

Extra-virgin olive oil

2 tablespoons maple syrup

Kosher salt and freshly ground black pepper

¾ teaspoon red pepper flakes

1 red onion, peeled and thinly sliced

12 fresh thyme sprigs

1 cup walnuts

2 medium (or 1 large) apple, cored and thinly sliced

Sea salt

VINAIGRETTE

3 tablespoons apple cider vinegar

3 tablespoons freshly squeezed lemon juice

1½ tablespoons Dijon mustard

2 tablespoons maple syrup

½ cup extra-virgin olive oil

Kosher salt and freshly ground black pepper

Preheat oven to 425°F. In a small bowl, cover golden raisins with hot water and let sit to plump.

On a baking sheet lined with foil, toss Brussels sprouts with 2 tablespoons olive oil, 2 tablespoons of the maple syrup, a pinch of kosher salt, a few grinds of black pepper, and the red pepper flakes. Spread the sprouts in an even layer and roast for 10 minutes, just until they start to soften but before they turn golden.

Add the red onion, thyme, and walnuts to the baking sheet. Toss everything together to combine, then spread in an even layer and roast for 10 more minutes, until the Brussels sprouts start to get golden and crispy on the edges.

While everything roasts, make the vinaigrette. Whisk together the apple cider vinegar, lemon juice, Dijon mustard, and maple syrup. Slowly whisk in the olive oil and season with kosher salt and black pepper to taste.

Drain the raisins and add them to the baking sheet with the apples. Toss everything together to combine, then return to the oven for just a few minutes so that everything warms through. Transfer to a serving bowl, toss with a small amount of the vinaigrette, and sprinkle everything with a bit of sea salt. Serve immediately. The vinaigrette will keep up to a week in the fridge.

(See photo on page 82.)

BOURBON AND BROWN SUGAR WHIPPED SWEET POTATOES

This is one of the easiest and most crowd-pleasing side dishes ever. Its sweetness is a subtle nod to the ol' marshmallow-topped sweet potatoes of Thanksgivings past, but this one skips the gooeyness in favor of bright citrus and warm bourbon. And its simplicity makes it perfect for delegating to the not-too-experienced-in-the-kitchen relative who wants to help out.

SERVES 8

3 large sweet potatoes, scrubbed

Zest and juice of 1 orange

¼ cup (packed) light brown sugar

2 tablespoons bourbon

4 tablespoons (½ stick) unsalted butter, at room temperature

Kosher salt and freshly ground black pepper

Preheat the oven to 425°F. Prick the sweet potatoes all over with a fork, wrap them in foil, and place them directly on the oven rack. Place a sheet of foil under the rack to catch any drips as the potatoes bake. Bake for 1 to 1½ hours, until a knife slides easily into the sweet potatoes with no resistance.

Let the sweet potatoes sit until cool enough to handle. Gently slip the sweet potato flesh out of the peels and into a medium bowl. Add the orange zest and juice, sugar, bourbon, butter, and a liberal pinch of salt and freshly ground black pepper and roughly mash.

Use a hand mixer to mix until very smooth and then add more brown sugar and salt as needed.

SAUSAGE, CHERRY, AND SAGE–STUFFED TURKEY BREAST

Though a whole roasted bird is traditional, I think that a turkey breast rolled up with stuffing is hands-down the most flavorful way to serve the bird on Thanksgiving. I ask my butcher to debone and butterfly the turkey breast so that the hard part's done before I bring it home. If you like, prepare the stuffing the night before and keep refrigerated until 30 minutes before prepping the turkey.

SERVES 8

½ cup dried cherries

½ cup port wine

6 tablespoons (¾ stick) unsalted butter

1 sweet onion, diced

1 celery stalk, diced

1 pound sweet Italian sausage, casings removed

¼ cup chopped pecans, toasted (see page 47)

1 tablespoon fresh thyme leaves

2 cups herb-seasoned stuffing mix (I like the classic version by Pepperidge Farm)

1 large egg, beaten

1 cup chicken broth

Kosher salt and freshly ground black pepper

1 whole (3- to 4-pound) turkey breast, deboned and butterflied

Herbes de Provence

Rosemary, thyme, and sage sprigs, for garnish

BITS OF BRILLIANCE:

This recipe makes more stuffing than will fit in the bird (and your guests are sure to want a big scoop of it on their plates), so pack the remaining stuffing into its own oven-safe dish, bake for the last hour with the turkey (at 325°F), and serve it on the buffet.

In a small saucepan, combine the dried cherries, port, and ¼ cup water. Bring to a boil over high heat, then turn the heat to low and simmer for 3 minutes. Set aside to cool.

In a medium skillet, melt 2 tablespoons of the butter over medium heat and add the onion and celery. Sauté for 5 minutes, or until the onion begins to soften, and then add the sausage. Cook, breaking it up with the back of a spoon, until the sausage is browned and cooked completely through. Add the pecans, thyme, and cherries with their cooking liquid. Cook for a few minutes, scraping up the browned bits from the bottom of the pan.

Transfer the mixture to a large bowl and add the stuffing mix, egg, broth, ¾ teaspoon salt, and several grinds of pepper. Stir to combine until the stuffing mix is consistently moistened.

Preheat the oven to 375°F. Place a baking rack over a foil-lined baking sheet.

Unfold the turkey onto a cutting board with the skin side down. Sprinkle with kosher salt and pepper and then spread the stuffing in an even layer, about ½ inch thick, all over the meat, but leaving a small border on each short side so the stuffing doesn't overflow when it's rolled up (see note about the extra stuffing).

Starting from a long end, roll the turkey into a tight cylinder. Cut 6-inch lengths of kitchen twine and tie around the turkey at 3-inch intervals to hold it all together. Carefully tuck any stray stuffing back into the turkey roll.

Place the turkey seam side down on the baking rack. Melt the remaining 4 tablespoons of butter and brush it over the turkey. Sprinkle generously with salt, pepper, and herbes de Provence. Roast for 1 hour and then lower the oven temperature to 325°F and roast for 1 more hour. The turkey is ready when a thermometer inserted into the center registers 150°F.

Remove the turkey from the oven, cover with foil, and let rest for 10 minutes before carving. Transfer to a platter or cutting board, cut into ¾-inch-thick slices, and garnish with lots of rosemary, thyme, and sage.

APRICOT AND CRANBERRY CHUTNEY

Cranberry sauce is good and all, but I've always had a sneaking suspicion that it could be a whole lot more interesting. This apricot and cranberry chutney proves it, packed full of savory flavors and the sweet, spicy kick of candied ginger. Serve it on a cheese plate, spread it on a baguette, and of course, pair it with the Thanksgiving turkey. Finally, a sauce worthy of crowning the bird!

SERVES 8

2½ cups frozen or fresh cranberries

1 cup apple cider vinegar

½ red onion, coarsely chopped

½ cup (packed) brown sugar, or to taste

½ cup dried apricots, coarsely chopped

2 tablespoons candied ginger, minced

½ teaspoon kosher salt

Bring all the ingredients to a low boil in a medium saucepan over medium-low heat. Turn the heat to the lowest setting, cover, and simmer for about 30 minutes, or until the berries just begin to burst.

Uncover and let simmer for 3 minutes or so, until the mixture thickens to your desired consistency. Cool to room temperature, or refrigerate in an airtight container for up to 1 week.

To make the decorative leaf cutout: Roll out the extra dough on a lightly floured surface. Use a cookie cutter, or better yet, find a pretty leaf outside and use it as a template. Lay the template on the dough and cut out the shape with the tip of a sharp knife and then place the cutout on a piece of aluminum foil. Sprinkle with sugar and bake alongside the tart until light golden brown (remove from the oven after about 20 minutes, or when it's golden brown). Place on top of the baked tart, and watch your guests fight over who gets to eat it!

MAPLE PECAN TART

Of all the dishes that find their way onto the Thanksgiving table year after year, my mom's pecan tart is the one that we all insist can never be varied. Its heavy dose of maple syrup tastes like pure autumn, and the minimal number of ingredients make it straightforwardly, simply great. In case you're wondering, I think it's totally fine to use a high-quality store-bought piecrust. Maybe it's because I'm more a fan of fillings than crust, but I like the consistency of knowing exactly what I'm going to get from a boxed piecrust . . . and for me at least, homemade pastry can be a challenge!

SERVES 8

Store-bought or homemade pie pastry to fill a 9-inch tart pan

1¾ cups lightly toasted coarsely chopped pecans (see page 47)

3 large eggs

1 cup pure maple syrup

2 tablespoons (¼ stick) unsalted butter, melted

2 teaspoons pure vanilla extract

¼ teaspoon salt

Pecan halves, for garnish (about 40)

Lightly sweetened whipped cream (optional)

Place an oven rack at the lowest position and set a baking sheet on the rack. Preheat the oven to 350°F.

On a lightly floured surface, roll out the pastry into an 11-inch circle. Carefully transfer the pastry to a 9-inch tart pan with a removable bottom. Press the dough into the top edge of the pan to remove the excess and then use the remaining dough to make a leaf cutout for the top of the tart (see note above for instructions).

In a medium bowl, whisk the eggs and then add the chopped pecans, maple syrup, butter, vanilla, and salt. Whisk to combine and then pour into the pastry shell. Line the edge of the tart with slightly overlapping pecan halves, if desired.

Place the tart pan on the preheated baking sheet and bake for 30 to 35 minutes, or until the filling is set and the pastry is lightly browned. Let cool in the pan on a wire rack. Remove the rim of the pan and place the tart, still on the pan bottom, on a serving platter.

Serve with whipped cream, if desired.

Bonjour

winter

capital letters and

A B C D E
G H
L

LAUREL & HEARTY

basic upper
lowercase alphabet,
the top of this page
ters that follow the
tice if you'll be calli
down each one into

CREATED BY JILL

lowercase alph

a · b · b · c · c
· e · f · f · g · g
· i · i · j · j
· l · l · m
· o · p · p · q
· s · s · t · t
· v · v · w

>>>>>>>>> EMBRACING THE SEASON <<<<<<<<<

SIGHTS, SOUNDS, AND TASTES OF WINTER

There's a certain magic that blows in with the first frost of winter, a bewitching feeling of remembrance that sends pleasant shivers down my spine as I bundle up against the crisp air. This is the season of ritual, as we look for ways to re-create the feelings we've felt during holidays past.

I'll forever associate winter with romance; it's the season when Adam and I fell in love and then, a year later, got engaged. He proposed just before Christmas, and a few days later we hopped on a flight to the English countryside where I met his mother's British family and explored the charming village where she grew up. It was exactly how you'd imagine a classic English Christmas—proper roast dinners at the

pub around the corner, darting into cafes to escape the bracing cold and warm up with a cuppa, lots of people gathered into a tiny house eating sticky toffee pudding. Our next stop was London, just the two of us. It was my first trip, and we bundled up in coats and scarves and took long walks from Buckingham Palace to the London Eye, soaking up the beauty of the city and our newly engaged status. I'll never forget standing on the balcony of the hotel, watching New Year's Eve fireworks go off above the Thames.

It's now become a tradition each year to wake up on the day after Thanksgiving and begin preparing our home and our senses for the coming months of custom and celebration.

Camille

HERE'S HOW I CONNECT WITH ALL THE SENSES TO USHER IN THE WINTER SEASON:

TEXTURE.

Soft velvet, cozy wool, luxurious cashmere—layering such tactile materials creates a sense of security, where one can truly come home to escape from the outside world. I transform the living room into a cozy haven with wool rugs that warm bare feet and faux fur throws tossed over armchairs and couches to encourage curling up and taking a post-holiday-meal afternoon nap. When getting dressed in the morning, think about materials that turn bundling up into a sensual experience—silk, cashmere, and angora pamper the skin while insulating from frigid air.

SCENT.

I think that there's no sensory experience more evocative of holiday memories than the aromatics of winter: wood burning in the fireplace, evergreen branches, and cinnamon wafting from the oven. So many of the season's fragrances are wrapped up in culinary delights, but even when I'm not preparing a holiday feast, I like to fill my house with cozy scents by burning a balsam fir candle and placing a gorgeous bottle of ginger soap next to the sink. I also bring in natural decorative elements that have the added bonus of delicious fragrance. A bay-leaf garland on the mantel, clove-studded oranges filling a bowl in the entryway, and a pine wreath on the door all impart the lovely scents of winter.

COLOR.

There are so many beautiful color palettes to choose from around the holidays: classic red and green, of course, but how about a bevy of jewel tones or a snowfall-inspired spectrum of whites? For me, there's something about metallics that captures the sparkling, glowing, and celebratory feel of the season, and I love to deck out my tree in every shade of silver, gold, and bronze. Whatever hues you prefer, when it comes to holiday decor, I'm a firm believer in choosing a palette and sticking to it, from the tree to the stockings to the table centerpiece. There's no better way to get a cohesive and "designed" look on a budget, and determining your palette before you begin to shop for decorations will help you achieve a well-edited selection of pieces that you'll look forward to unpacking again year after year.

TASTE.

'Tis the season to eat, drink, and be merry! As much as I love experimenting with new recipes and innovative flavors, there's something about the winter months that just calls for the comfort foods of childhood and the familiar flavors that always make an appearance on the holiday table. For me, Christmas morning goes hand in hand with my mom's fresh-from-the-oven almond kringle, and now that I have a daughter, I'm looking for ways to be intentional about creating new family taste traditions of our own. Think about how you feel when you come in from the cold and are handed a steaming mug of spicy cider, or sit down for Christmas dinner to a table groaning with roasted meats and bottles of red wine. Although I often can't help myself from adding one new item to the menu each year, I know that keeping these beloved traditions alive is sacred. And of course, one of my very favorite tastes of the season? Fizzy Champagne as glasses clink on New Year's Eve!

13

SETTING THE WINTER TABLE

Some of my favorite holiday memories center around setting the table in preparation for a family feast. When I was little, my mom would let me craft place cards for the Thanksgiving table; I'd use my best cursive and colored pencils to scrawl each guest's name and a little reminder of one thing we had to be thankful for. A few days before Christmas, we'd unpack my mom's china adorned with evergreen trees and reindeer, which seemed even more special owing to its limited use. These days, I still get a rush from designing a holiday table that feels different from the year before, one that brings delight to family and friends the moment they lay eyes on the festive linen tablecloth, delicate vintage glassware, or flickering candlelight. A beautiful table contributes to the magical feeling in the air and creates all kinds of anticipation for the feast ahead. This year, I incorporated shimmering touches and metallic accents to cast a warm glow over my holiday table, inviting guests to eat, drink, and be merry until long after the sun goes down.

Camille

PALETTE.

Evergreen, ivory, and burnished gold.

LINENS.

In an effort to let the beauty of my vintage wood table shine, I topped it simply with a linen runner and a second "runner" formed from evergreen branches. During the holidays, I look for ways to incorporate as much greenery as possible—nothing's more evocative of a classic Christmas than pine, cedar, and fir (and the wonderful scents that they impart!). No need to craft any kind of complicated garland—to achieve this look, simply cut branches to size and lay them artfully around the centerpiece.

CENTERPIECE.

I've always had a bit of an obsession with *croquembouches*—the tree-shaped French confections consisting of towering stacks of cream puffs, "glued" together with caramel. Sure, you could spend hours in the kitchen making pastry from scratch and then methodically assembling the tree . . . or you *could* order one from a great local bakery (my preferred route!). Either way, something this tall and dramatic is all the centerpiece your holiday table will need.

When there's no room for flowers on the table, I often consider adding a few blooms or branches in another spot, like a side table or buffet. For this look, my friend and floral designer Elizabeth Lewis gathered simple bunches into mercury glass vases, and we arranged them on the mantel directly behind the table for a stunning display. These included ranunculus, tulips, winter berries, and bay leaves.

PLACE SETTINGS.

Since my everyday dishes are made of casual stoneware, the sheer sight of fine china on the table transforms any dinner into a special occasion. The woven pattern on these plates feels modern while the gold accents add glamour and sparkle, especially when illuminated by candlelight. I love the vintage vibe of the etched Champagne coupes and mismatched silverware, adding a timeless touch that recalls Christmases of long ago.

THE DETAILS.

A scattering of narrow brass candlesticks in varying heights appears to dance across the length of the table. I scooped these up at a thrift store recently and have been surprised by their versatility—they've been the perfect finishing detail on loads of different tabletop looks, and their slender silhouettes add a certain gracefulness.

On the first holiday I ever spent with them, Adam's British side of the family introduced me to the tradition of Christmas crackers. A cardboard tube is filled with treats and wrapped in pretty paper, then placed at each setting, ready to be opened at Christmas dinner. These do double duty as place cards, with each guest's name calligraphied across the front of the packaging.

SOURCES

Floral design: The Nouveau Romantics
Calligraphy: Mia Carameros
Props: Loot Vintage Rentals
China: Vera Wang Gilded Weave
Dinnerware/Newlywish
Croquembouche: Word of Mouth Catering

HOW TO ADD A VINTAGE, HANDMADE TOUCH TO THE TABLE

Rhoda and Anna of Loot Vintage Rentals

1 | To add loads of character to a table setting, we encourage mixing sets of china, glassware, and flatware together. The key is making sure there's one cohesive element that runs throughout each place setting to tie it all together: a napkin, place card, or other decorative element will do the trick nicely.

2 | Anything can be incorporated into a tabletop, so think outside the china cabinet! Instead of limiting your centerpiece to vases or candles, use generous quantities of unexpected items strewn across the center of the table for excitement. Collection of snow globes acquired from holidays past? Abundance of yarn balls in the attic? Have fun with it!

3 | Using uncommon objects as vessels or candlesticks is a creative way to surprise your guests. Flowers look beautiful in vintage wood cheese boxes, brass goblets, china sugar bowls, or glass decanters. Taper candles are really lovely displayed in old bottles, vintage spools, and industrial gears.

4 | Vintage textiles add so much interest to a tabletop—no need for them to be actual tablecloths. Antique flour or grain sacks can be torn and repurposed as runners or napkins. Try layering different patterns together for a rich, textured look.

5 | Get inspired by nature and look for ways to bring the outdoors in. Antlers, rocks, stumps, leaves, or twigs can all have beautiful shapes and textures and can be personalized with paint, glitter, or string. Use the right size drill bit to bore holes in wooden pieces for instant candelabras!

14

THE PARTY-READY PANTRY

My favorite kind of entertaining is the laid-back, no-fuss variety—inviting a few friends over for dinner, opening a bottle of wine while I put together a few simple but delicious dishes, and sitting down to enjoy the meal with my friends, feeling neither worn out nor frazzled. Creating such an easygoing atmosphere is the direct result of preparation on the front end, and the extra effort to get organized pays dividends come party time. One of the greatest tools a prepared hostess can have in her arsenal is a well-stocked pantry. It gives me peace of mind to know that if last-minute guests stop by for drinks or even dinner, I can rustle up something scrumptious. And if the idea of hosting a dinner party after a

demanding workday makes you break out in hives, just imagine that your kitchen is so well stocked that all you need from the grocery store on the way home is a few salmon fillets and veggies for a salad.

So what are the items I reach for constantly, the ones I could *never* live without in my kitchen? Garlic, olive oil, herbes de Provence—they're standbys that I reach for on an almost daily basis and that never let me down. But there's also a new guard rising up in my kitchen, ingredients like Maldon sea salt and fish sauce that are fairly recent yet equally essential additions to my pantry shelves. Here are a handful of the items that are fundamental to my cooking, both for multicourse dinner parties and weeknight family meals.

Camille

GARLIC.

I don't think I could live without garlic's punchy, addictive flavor—it's a must-have in just about every type of cuisine from Italian to French to Vietnamese. Avoid buying the prechopped or prepeeled garlic—this is one time when it pays to go the fresh route, even if it requires a teensy bit more work.

LEMONS.

Thank goodness for our Meyer lemon tree growing in the backyard, which saves me who-knows-how-much money at the grocery store! I use lemons to infuse pitchers of water, brighten up rich sauces, and garnish fish and poultry dishes. And the peel is a must-have for baked goods, salad dressings, and sprinkling over roasted veggies for a zesty finish.

SRIRACHA SAUCE.

Its sweet and spicy flavor is the secret ingredient that gives so many of my dishes their kick. I use it in place of red pepper flakes when sautéing vegetables and mix a bit of it with mayo for a perfect quick aioli to spread on sandwiches or serve with steamed artichokes.

NUTS AND SEEDS.

My mom always taught me to keep pecans, walnuts, and almonds in the freezer, which prevents them from spoiling so they're always at the ready for an impromptu batch of cookies or a satisfying snack. She also taught me that nuts are infinitely better when toasted—the gentle heat boosts flavor and adds a great crunch that takes them to a whole new level. My freezer shelves always include her mainstays, plus pistachios, hazelnuts, and Marcona almonds.

MALDON SEA SALT.

If you ask me, Maldon deserves its own category separate from other salts. It's *that* good. A sprinkling of these large, gorgeous flakes over veggies (cooked or raw) takes them to an entirely different stratosphere.

HERBES DE PROVENCE.

I usually have several varieties of dried herbs on hand, but this classic Provençal mixture, which includes fennel, basil, lavender, and thyme (among other things), is hands down my favorite for adding herbal flavor to soups, roasted meats, and sautéed vegetables.

EXTRA-VIRGIN OLIVE OIL.

You *could* stock loads of different oils in your pantry—coconut, canola, flaxseed, peanut, sesame, and sunflower are just a few of the most popular—or you could do what I do and use a good-quality, moderately priced extra-virgin olive oil for almost everything! Yes, every oil has its own slightly different flavor (and when I'm making an Asian stir-fry, nothing beats the nutty taste of sesame oil), but 99 percent of the time, extra-virgin olive just gets the job done, and more tastily than almost anything else.

BALSAMIC VINEGAR.

I keep a little squeeze bottle of reduced balsamic in my pantry at all times to drizzle over salads and even complement sweet dishes, like strawberries with a scoop of vanilla ice cream (seriously, try it!). To make your own balsamic reduction, pour an inexpensive bottle of balsamic vinegar into a nonreactive metal pan over medium-high heat. Let it come to a boil, then reduce to low and let simmer for 30 minutes, until a spoon dipped into the vinegar gets lightly coated with a syrupy consistency. When it's almost as thick as honey, pull it off the heat—it'll thicken a bit more as it cools. It'll keep in the pantry for up to 1 month.

MAPLE SYRUP.

So much more than a topping for pancakes and waffles, maple syrup is my go-to sweetener for just about everything from salad dressing to meat marinades to muffins. It adds a certain depth of flavor that gives it secret-ingredient

status in my ingredient arsenal. My favorite way to roast vegetables? Just toss them with olive oil, kosher salt, herbs, and a little maple syrup, and roast at 400°F for 30 minutes. I swear—butternut squash becomes like candy!

CERIGNOLA OLIVES.

There's something about the meaty texture and briny flavor of Cerignolas that's just . . . mind blowing. I like all kinds of olives and often incorporate them into cheese plates or pasta dishes, but when I've got Cerignolas and a glass of Pinot Grigio in hand, I can easily polish off a bowl of these myself before dinner.

RED PEPPER FLAKES.

I like a bit of kick in my dishes, especially when it's combined with other flavors to create that satisfying marriage of sweet and spicy. Try adding a pinch to broccoli or kale just before roasting or sprinkle on popcorn with a bit of sugar, salt, and cinnamon. Just remember: a little goes a *long* way.

DIJON MUSTARD.

One of my very favorite salad dressings is made with 1 part Dijon, 1 part honey, 2 parts olive oil, and a squeeze of lemon juice. It's just about as good as it gets. Dijon is also a must-have ingredient for marinades and simple pan sauces to accompany meat or fish, and it's my favorite sandwich condiment. I love the brand Maille for its balanced flavor and creamy texture.

CHICKPEAS AND OTHER BEANS.

I think high-quality canned beans that have been rinsed well are every bit as good as their dried counterparts, and they're infinitely quicker to prepare. Chickpeas are essential for making hummus, and I always have a variety of beans on hand for adding to soups, salads, chili, and last-minute appetizers.

RAW HONEY.

We go through a *lot* of honey at our house. It's a healthier alternative to processed sugars and adds a balanced sweetness to smoothies, baked goods, and salad dressings. I love to serve it with sliced pears and blue cheese for the *best* three-ingredient appetizer, and a drizzle of honey over Greek yogurt and berries is my favorite way to start the day.

DRIED FRUIT.

Aside from roasted almonds, dried fruit is my most frequent midday nibble. I love tossing dried cherries in salads, sweet apricots into bran muffins, and golden raisins into sautéed broccoli or kale (really, it's amazing!). The key is soaking them, which completely transforms a raisin into something so juicy and sweet that it's almost unrecognizable from its former dried-up self. Just cover any kind of dried fruit with warm water, orange juice, or even sweet wine, let it hang out for 20 minutes or so, then drain!

FRESH HERBS.

Nothing does more to punch up the flavors of your cooking than using fresh herbs! I always keep three or four varieties on hand—winter pastas call for a few torn sage leaves; parsley adds a touch of brightness to roasted meats; and in Japanese or Thai dishes I might combine cilantro, mint, and basil and shower the entire thing with fresh, zesty flavor! If you have the inclination to grow fresh herbs at home, I can't recommend it highly enough. In the winter when my herbs are dormant, I pick up fresh herbs from the grocery store or farmers' market, then store by placing them in a couple inches of cold water in a glass and storing them on a middle shelf in my fridge.

CHEESE.

It may not be a revolutionary idea, but there's no doubt that setting out a couple varieties of great cheeses with some wine is the perfect way to kick off a dinner party or sate guests' appetites during cocktail hour. I store at least a couple of fantastic cheeses in my fridge at all times—it goes a long way in helping me feel prepared for impromptu guests or even a cozy evening by the fire with just the three of us! To help cheese last as long as possible, wrap it in parchment paper (plastic wrap can impart flavors and chemicals into the cheese), label with the variety and date, and then place in the warmest part of your fridge, like the cheese or vegetable drawer.

EGGS.

There are eggs . . . and there are organic, farm-fresh eggs with deep yellow yolks and a certain richness you just don't get from the supermarket variety. I pick up a dozen every weekend at the farmers' market, and on those nights when I can't think of what to make for dinner, a fluffy omelet with a sprinkling of cheddar and a few sautéed veggies always does the trick.

AVOCADOS.

Avocados are like that enviable woman who seems to be able to do it all: they're creamy, delicious, incredibly good for you, and paired with a few halved cherry tomatoes and a liberal dose of sea salt, they can serve as a light meal on their own. In the mornings, I top toasted bread with a smear of avocado and squeeze of lemon juice; for lunch, I add a healthy dose of protein to all-veggie salads with a few big chunks; and at dinnertime, sliced avocados top soups, fill tacos, and become a rich sandwich condiment.

GUITTARD CHOCOLATE WAFERS.

There are so many great chocolates for baking on the market now, but my mom recently made what we all pronounced to be "the best chocolate chip cookies in the history of the world," and the only thing we could credit it to was the inclusion of semisweet Guittard chocolate chips. Since then, I've been buying up these wafers, which are perfect for melting into a silky-smooth chocolate sauce or simply nibbling on as an after-dinner treat.

THE BEST CHOCOLATE CHIP COOKIES EVER

MAKES 18 LARGE COOKIES

1½ cups all-purpose flour

1 teaspoon baking powder

½ teaspoon kosher salt

¼ teaspoon baking soda

8 tablespoons (1 stick) unsalted butter, at room temperature

1 cup (packed) light brown sugar

½ cup granulated sugar

2 large egg yolks

1 large egg

2 teaspoons pure vanilla extract

8 ounces semisweet or bittersweet chocolate chips (high quality is a must here—I use Guittard)

Maldon sea salt

Place racks in upper and lower thirds of the oven and preheat the oven to 375°F. Cover 2 baking sheets with parchment paper and set aside.

Whisk the flour, baking powder, salt, and baking soda in a medium bowl; set aside.

In the bowl of an electric mixer, beat the butter, brown sugar, and granulated sugar on medium-high speed until light and fluffy, 3 to 4 minutes. Add the egg yolks, egg, and vanilla. Beat, occasionally scraping down the sides of the bowl, until the mixture is pale and fluffy. Reduce the mixer speed to the lowest setting and slowly add the flour mixture, mixing just to blend. Use a spatula to fold in the chocolate.

Spoon rounded tablespoonfuls of cookie dough onto the prepared baking sheets, spacing them at least 1 inch apart. Sprinkle the cookies liberally with sea salt.

Bake the cookies, rotating the sheets halfway through, until just golden brown around the edges, about 12 minutes (the cookies will firm up as they cool). Let cool slightly on baking sheets and then transfer to wire racks. Let cool completely.

15

LITTLE LUXURIES

Last night, I got into a spat with Adam and was left feeling sapped of energy; although we'd resolved things, I just couldn't seem to get out of my funk. After putting Phoebe to bed, I went into the bathroom, shut the door, and ran a very hot bath. A few drops of rose oil and my favorite lavender-scented candle enhanced the spa-like atmosphere, and I slathered on a face mask and sank into the water all the way up to my shoulders . . . then just lay there for a while. It's amazing how a luxurious bath and even just fifteen minutes of deep relaxation can cure a host of ills—or at least improve your outlook! It's so important to take some time to think about which simple treats buoy your spirits and make you feel most pampered, whether it's going out for a great dinner, heading to yoga class, or just spending some time solo. Having a few tried-and-true stress relievers to draw upon when you need a boost is crucial, especially in the long darker months of winter when we're a bit more deprived of the mood-lifting benefits of sunshine. And the best thing about these "little luxuries" is that they're more about quality than quantity; you don't need to spend a fortune in order to feel like a million bucks. Here are my favorites—my hope is that you'll use these as a springboard as you start building a list of the things that are most nurturing to *your* spirit!

Camille

1. THE HIGHEST-QUALITY COFFEE BEANS I CAN GET MY HANDS ON.

Almost nothing brings me greater joy than a cup of just-brewed coffee when I first wake up (and if you think I'm exaggerating . . . I'm not). Independent roasters around the country have elevated coffee to an art form over the past few years, and when I order great-quality beans and grind them fresh at home, my daily routine feels like an occasion worth celebrating.

2. SUBSCRIPTIONS TO MAGAZINES THAT INSPIRE ME.

I get loads of new ideas and inspiration from magazines across all different categories: interiors, food, travel, wellness, and fashion. Ordering monthly subscriptions is not only way more cost-effective than buying single issues at the store; it also ensures that I have a regular dose of inspiration delivered to my doorstep.

3. GREAT CHEESE.

Bonus points if it's one I've never tried before! It feels like such a treat to stop by my local cheese shop on my way home and try a few selections from the case, and I usually take home a really stinky blue and eat it with water crackers and a few slices of pear.

4. BEAUTIFUL HAND SOAP IN THE KITCHEN.

I've tried just about every different brand of hand soap out there, and I always go back to the glass bottles of beautifully scented soap by La Compagnie de Provence that double as countertop decoration and a little touch that makes cleaning up after dinner more fun.

5. MANICURES.

I used to always do my own nails, but since my schedule of cooking, crafting, and caring for a baby means almost instantaneous chipping, I've started splurging on biweekly professional shellac manicures that stay perfect for at least ten days. It's amazing what having well-groomed nails does for my overall sense of well-being, and the mini-massage that I get on each visit is worth its weight in gold.

6. CHANEL LIPSTICK.

I may not own one of the brand's classic handbags or tweed jackets (maybe someday!), but I can still experience a bit of its *très chic* allure by scooping up one of the rose-scented lipsticks in a new shade of the season. Every time I slick one on, I feel instantly more glamorous. (Even when I'm simultaneously dabbing baby food off my blouse!)

7. BATH OILS AND SCENTED LOTIONS.

I've already waxed poetic about my love of a hot bath, and the experience is taken to a new level by adding a few drops of rose-scented oil while the water's running. After I dry off, I slather on generous amounts of great-smelling lotion, which is especially nourishing for dry winter skin.

8. ABUNDANT PRODUCE FROM THE FARMERS' MARKET.

Sure, it's probably a bit more expensive than your grocery store fare, and you may not have an *exact* plan for that huge bunch of striped beets or kohlrabi, but few things bring me more joy than unloading my farmers' market tote and filling my kitchen with colorful, healthy produce from nearby farms.

9. PRETTY NOTEBOOKS AND REALLY GOOD PENS.

As a blogger, I'm on my computer for hours each day, so pulling out a beautiful notebook with a hard cover and grid-lined paper and brainstorming ideas with a fine-point black pen forces me to slow down and take some extra time. And since I'm almost always typing on a keyboard, it's good for me to practice my handwriting once in a while, too!

10. FRESH FLOWERS.

Almost every weekend, I bring home a fresh bunch from the flower market—hydrangeas, peonies, and garden roses are my personal favorites, although when springtime rolls around, nothing thrills me more than an oversize glass jar full of blooming branches on the dining table. See pages 25 and 181 for tips on living with flowers through the seasons.

16

BOTTOMS UP!

>>>>>>>> A FEW WINTER COCKTAILS <<<<<<<<

If you typically relegate cocktails to summer months, then you're long overdue to experience the unmatched pleasure of spending a winter's night sipping hot toddies by the fire or taking refuge from the frigid temps by cozying up to a dimly lit bar with a whisky sour. Not to mention the fact that the holiday season is brimming with opportunities for festive sipping—Christmas parties, holiday open houses, and New Year's Eve fetes can certainly be fueled by bottles of wine, but where's the fun in that? At our annual company party, no matter how big a batch of holiday punch I mix up, it never fails that by the end of the night the only thing left in my gigantic punch bowl are a few lone slices of oranges and grapefruit.

There's no better way to get people mingling and having a good time!

When it comes to mixing drinks, I've learned that the easiest recipes often turn out to be the ones that guests can't stop raving about. I typically limit my ingredient list to three to five items, many of which I always keep on hand, so that I'm able to relax with my guests instead of playing bartender all night. That's why you won't find any recipes in this section that require fancy mixology skills—if you can follow a few simple steps, you'll be making these drinks like a pro! And you just might discover the one that's destined to be your new "signature" cocktail. Feel free to take all the credit.

Camille

ELDERFLOWER GINGER FIZZ

St-Germain is quite possibly the most elegant-looking bottle on my liqueur shelf, but since it's been made in Paris from elderberry flowers by the same company since 1884, would you really expect anything less? Typically mixed with Champagne, it contains hints of stone fruit and citrus. Here I've turned up the flavor on this classic cocktail with a kick of ginger and a colorful cherry garnish.

SERVES 1

1½ ounces St-Germain

1 ounce ginger syrup

½ ounce lemon juice

4 ounces Champagne or other sparkling wine

2 maraschino cherries (look for the Luxardo brand—it's pricey but known among bartenders as the "king" of maraschino cherries)

Pour the St-Germain into a Champagne flute. Add the ginger syrup and lemon juice and stir to combine. Top with Champagne and garnish with the maraschino cherries.

ORCHARD PUNCH

I mix up a big batch of fruity, boozy punch at my company holiday party every year. This year, I quadrupled the recipe and still had to make a second batch to satisfy, ahem, thirsty guests! This one's brimming with the cozy flavors of cider and spices, using apples and their juice in three different ways. And the best thing about punch? Guests can help themselves to seconds without having to ask!

SERVES 6

½ 750 ml bottle sweet Riesling

1 red apple, cored and sliced

1 green apple, cored and sliced

1 cup apple juice

2 tablespoons lemon juice

750 ml hard apple cider

Whole star anise

Pour the Riesling into a large pitcher and then add the apples, apple juice, and lemon juice. Let marinate in the fridge for at least 1 hour and up to 4 hours.

Just before serving, add the cider and divide equally among ice-filled highball glasses. Garnish with star anise and serve.

TOASTED ALMOND COFFEE

Is it a drink, or is it dessert? When it's chilly outside and you're holding a mug of this amaretto-spiked coffee, who really cares! This drink is undeniably cozy, and the cream makes it decadent (just don't tell the dieters in the group that it's in there!). After the dinner plates are cleared and I've settled into that blissful postmeal relaxation mode, there's nothing I'd rather be sipping on.

SERVES 1

1 shot plus 1 teaspoon amaretto liqueur

1 teaspoon agave syrup

⅓ cup heavy whipping cream

½ teaspoon confectioners' sugar

6 ounces hot brewed coffee

Chocolate shavings

1 cinnamon stick

In a heatproof mug, combine 1 shot of amaretto and the agave syrup. Stir to dissolve.

In a chilled bowl, beat the cream on high until soft peaks form. Add 1 teaspoon amaretto and the confectioners' sugar and beat just to combine.

Pour the coffee into the amaretto and agave mixture and stir. Top with the whipped cream and chocolate shavings. Garnish with a cinnamon stick.

WINTER CITRUS GIMLET

I was first introduced to the joys of a classic gimlet at a mixology class a couple of years ago, and its addictive sweetness combined with the clean flavor of the gin made it, well, a little too easy to drink! Since lime juice feels rather summery, I swapped it out for the winter oranges that fill my refrigerator shelves at this time of year. Garnished with fresh mint and citrus wheels, it's as pretty as it is refreshing.

SERVES 1

4 mint leaves

1 ounce light agave nectar

2 ounces fresh-squeezed orange juice (I love Cara Cara or blood oranges, both at their peak in the winter months!)

2 ounces gin

Fresh mint sprig

2 orange slices

In a cocktail shaker, muddle the mint leaves with the agave nectar and juice. Add the gin and fill to the top with ice. Cover and shake well.

Strain into an ice-filled old-fashioned glass and garnish with the mint and orange slices. Serve with a swizzle stick.

17

CREATING HOLIDAY TRADITIONS

It never fails: every winter, I'm going about my business as usual and not feeling the slightest bit holiday-ish, when something happens. I hear "Jingle Bell Rock" at a store while I'm shopping, or I bite into a piece of spicy gingerbread, and suddenly I feel an unexpected burst of Christmas spirit. What is it about certain sights, scents, and sounds that stirs up festive feelings and makes even the Scroogiest among us want to spread good cheer?

Much of it has to do with the memories we associate with holidays past and the ones that we build upon to create newer traditions with the people we love. When someone asks me to name my favorite Christmas gifts I received as a child, I can honestly recall only two or three of them. But ask me about my favorite Christmas memories? Baking cookies with my mom, opening one special gift on Christmas Eve, going to see *The Nutcracker* at the ballet—the list goes on and on. With that in mind, I've started making an effort to prioritize creating and fostering traditions instead of buying loads of presents to wrap up under the tree. After all, cherished memories are some of the very best gifts we can give the people we love! Following are a few ideas for creating lasting ones that will infuse the holiday season with loads of fun.

MAKING HOME A HOLIDAY HAVEN

At our house, the holiday season kicks off the day we bring home our Christmas tree and start decking the halls. There's nothing more comforting than walking through my front door at the end of a workday and being greeted by a blazing fire, sparkling tree, and holiday music coming through the speakers. Here are a few ways that I make my home feel like the heart of the festivities each year.

TRIM THE TREE.

For as long as I can remember, I've anxiously anticipated bringing our big box of ornaments down from the attic and carefully unwrapping each one to hang on the tree. We turn on holiday tunes, pour mugs of rich cocoa topped with plenty of marshmallows, and get to work. Later that night, we'll watch classic movies with bowls of popcorn as we savor the sight of our decked-out tree twinkling in the background.

CREATE A MEANINGFUL ORNAMENT COLLECTION.

Growing up, my parents would buy my brother, sister, and me one new ornament each year. It was always personal—I might receive a teacup or a ballerina, depending on my age and interests—and by the time I'd grown up I had an array of special ornaments representing every holiday since my birth.

READ TOGETHER.

There are so many beautiful Christmas books—*The Gift of the Magi, A Christmas Carol, The Polar Express*—and during the holiday season I stack them in a basket by the fire for our family to read together in the evening. I love that as Phoebe grows up she'll begin associating Christmas with these classic tales!

CREATE FOOD MEMORIES

Let's face it: some of our most important traditions revolve around food, and the holidays probably wouldn't feel the same without a few certain dishes on the table. Every family has their own culinary traditions reflecting their background and heritage, and making and eating them together can be one of the most joyous ways to celebrate what makes your family a unique mix!

LET EVERYONE OWN PART OF THE MENU.

My English mother-in-law makes the best roast beef with horseradish sauce and Yorkshire pudding this side of the Atlantic, and it's always the centerpiece to our Christmas dinner. My mom shapes her famous loaf of almond kringle into a heart every Christmas morning. My aunt Leslie bakes amazing Christmas cookies and gives each member of the family a tin that's perfectly customized to their taste (mincemeat or chocolate chip, with or without pecans). It's fun when everyone has a specialty they look forward to making (and everyone else looks forward to eating!) each year.

BUILD A GINGERBREAD HOUSE.

As soon as Phoebe's old enough to help me decorate, I can't wait to let our creativity run wild as we construct little edible houses!

MAKE IT FEEL LIKE HOME FOR THOSE WHO ARE FAR AWAY.

It can be tough to be away from immediate family during the holidays, and as our family grows and my siblings' spouses join us for celebrations here in Austin, I look for ways to incorporate some of their families' food traditions into the menu. This year, I'll add a Cajun influence into a couple of our dishes so that my sister's Louisiana-bred new husband will get to taste a little bit of home!

EMBRACE HOLIDAY EXPERIENCES

There are so many fun activities happening during the holidays, and as booked as we get with our usual traditions, it's worth it to take a look around and consider a new experience that may become a favorite tradition in the years to come. Of course, it requires a little extra effort to bundle everyone up and make a trek to somewhere that might feel outside your comfort zone, but once you're there you won't regret a single moment.

GO SEE *THE NUTCRACKER*.

Every year growing up, my mom and grandmother would take my sister and me to see a performance of *The Nutcracker* ballet. The symphony music, graceful movements of the dancers, and sparkling set design left an indelible impression, and I can't wait to continue this tradition with my own children.

LOOK AT THE LIGHTS.

Austin has a famous display of lavish Christmas light creations called Trail of Lights, and every year thousands of people head downtown to take it all in. But no matter where you live, there will be streets in your town where the neighbors go all out and turn it into a wonderland. Pack thermoses of cocoa and tune in to the holiday station on the radio or pop on your favorite playlist, and then spend an evening driving around and viewing the glittering display.

BRIGHTEN THE HOLIDAYS FOR OTHERS.

There's no better time of year to start a tradition of service, and the holidays present many meaningful ways to give—both our time and our resources. Our family has always participated in a program called Operation Christmas Child, in which you choose a child of a certain age, fill a shoebox with gifts—both necessities and toys—and drop it off to be shipped with other boxes to impoverished countries around the world. Volunteer at a soup kitchen, pull a stocking on a giving tree, join carolers at a nursing home. As much of a cliché as it may be, the act of giving is really the best gift of all.

THE DOS AND DON'TS OF SENDING HOLIDAY CARDS

I love sending cards each year—it's the perfect time to pen a simple note to the people I care about, many of whom live far away. But all too often the act of sending cards can be fraught with stress (yet another thing to check off the to-do list at this busy time of year!). Here are a few dos and don'ts to make this year's card-sending process the most joyful yet.

1 | **DON'T** *brag. If you're sending a newsletter-style card, it's great to include exciting info about members of the family, but don't make it all about trophies, wins, and bragging rights. The goal here is not to impress the recipients on your list but rather to share the experiences and opportunities for growth that made the year unforgettable.*

2 | **DO** *include a photo (but only if you want). People love to see how members of your family have changed over the year. Whether your son shot up four inches or your husband decided to grow a beard, it's a great chance to give everyone a visual update. Before Adam and I had kids, we always sent cards with a cool design and meaningful message, but now that Phoebe's on the scene, I've realized how much our recipients love a card with a photo so they can follow along with her growth each year.*

3 | **DON'T** *overshare. Since the gesture of sending holiday cards is all about spreading joy and love, it's usually not the place to vent grievances, make a big political statement, or announce a major health issue. Keep it real, but focus on the positive.*

4 | **DO** *proofread all envelopes and greetings. Even if it means having someone else edit your work, try to avoid misspelling anyone's name.*

5 | **DON'T** *put too much pressure on yourself. I used to think that I had to hand address every single envelope, since I thought it looked so much prettier than printing out the labels. The problem was that by the time I finished writing over a hundred names and addresses, my hand was cramping and my brain was so fried that I had no energy left to write "Love, Camille," much less something more personal. Since this time of year can be so busy, it's really important to prioritize what's most important to you . . . and let the rest go. This year, I decided that I wanted to send a short, personal note with each of my cards, so I opted to get my addresses printed on the envelopes. Problem solved!*

6 | **DO** *start early! Sending out cards takes time, so in order to avoid a stress-fest or staying up until two o'clock in the morning to stamp and seal, start the process earlier than you think you need to. I have a tradition of getting most of my cards written, addressed, and ready for mailing during the long Thanksgiving weekend. When everyone's settled into their turkey coma, I curl up in front of the fire with my cards and a cup of tea—such a soothing ritual to kick off the holiday season.*

18

A COZY GAME NIGHT

A few years ago, a friend brought the game Catchphrase to a dinner party at my house. I eyed the box warily as it sat quietly on a sideboard through cocktails and dinner; after all, I didn't consider myself to be much of a "games person." Toward the end of the night, as I brewed coffee and brought out the flourless chocolate cake for dessert, someone suggested we move things to the living room, divide into teams, and give Catchphrase a whirl. And that's when the *real* party started. Suddenly, polite conversation became competitive sparring and I saw a whole new side to my normally well-behaved friends. Players shrieked in victory, someone's wineglass

toppled over, and I realized that the evening had turned into one of the most fun parties I'd ever hosted *or* attended.

Since then, hosting a game night for friends has become one of my favorite ways to spend an evening, especially as the weather turns cold and there's nowhere I'd rather be than curled up in front of the fire with my most fun-loving pals. And it's really as simple as making (or buying) a few snacks, pouring the cocktails, and settling in to watch the evening unfold. Feel free to let a last-minute phone call or friendly e-mail take the place of a "proper" invitation; after all, when it comes to hosting this kind of party, spontaneity's the name of the game.

Camille

The
MENU

A COZY GAME NIGHT

When guests are focused on dealing cards and rolling dice, food should be easy to pick up and eat—no knife and fork required. Finger foods like crostini and spiced nuts or bites served on small wooden skewers do the trick nicely. And so that the hostess can unwind with her guests, serve mostly room-temperature items that can hang out on a sideboard or table nearby, allowing everyone to help themselves between rounds. I love giving all my party menus a theme so that the flavors really complement each other, but going with a "game" motif seems a bit too cutesy. (Just say no to domino cookies and spade-shaped finger sandwiches!) Instead I got inspired by the exotic detailing on the vintage game table I borrowed from one of the guests and took a cue from its Middle Eastern engravings to create a menu of Moroccan-inflected hors d'oeuvres.

TO DRINK	ON THE COCKTAIL BUFFET TABLE	SOMETHING SWEET
MOROCCAN MANDARIN PUNCH, PAGE 136, AND MIDDLE EASTERN BEERS	CERIGNOLA OLIVES	ASSORTMENT OF OLD-FASHIONED CANDIES
MOROCCAN ROSE TEA, PAGE 136	POPCORN WITH RAS EL HANOUT, PAGE 137	
	SPICED NUTS WITH CURRANTS AND APRICOTS, PAGE 138	
	CARROT SOUP WITH CUMIN AND GINGER, PAGE 139	
	TANDOORI CHICKEN SKEWERS WITH YOGURT-HARISSA DIPPING SAUCE, PAGE 141	

GET THE LOOK

Since this party is all about creating a cozy and casual atmosphere for fun, keep the decor low-key by using items you already own to create a little Moroccan ambience. I pulled a low-slung coffee table into the center of the living room and surrounded it with floor cushions and poufs for lounging. There's no better way to encourage guests to kick off their heels and stay awhile! Don't be afraid to experiment with patterns you might not normally place side by side; you just might discover a striking combination. Embrace the interplay of varied textures to provide a sense of richness and warmth.

FIVE-MINUTE CENTERPIECE

Using a pretty bowl or urn, pile clementines or other citrus fruit into a pyramid to place in the center of the buffet table. Tuck sprigs of fresh mint or greenery in the spaces to add color and echo some of the exotic flavors in the menu, and a few whole cloves stuck into the fruit add an alluringly spicy fragrance. An added benefit? Guests can pull the sweet, juicy fruit straight from the centerpiece when it's time for dessert!

HOUSE OF CARDS

As a subtle nod to the gaming theme, I dressed up white linen cocktail napkins with some simple embroidery. To create your own, use a pencil to lightly trace the shape of your design and then fill in with freehand stitches using a needle and bright-colored thread. Voilà! Such a pretty detail that can be used again and again for game nights to come.

And here's a checklist of the supplies you'll want to have on hand to be fully prepared for any game night. I like to stash them all in a cool vintage box so they're ready to go at a moment's notice.

Notebooks
Pencils
Deck of cards
Dice
Timer

THE GAMES

It's nice to have a varied selection of games available so that guests can weigh in on what they're in the mood to play. If you have lots of players, set up two stations on opposite ends of the room so that more than one match can happen at once. Here are some classics that are always a hit:

Dominoes: Fun for all ages with a retro vibe
Backgammon: An intense game of strategy—great for your intellectual friends
Catchphrase: My favorite for a party, since it's easy to learn and always seems to result in hilarity
Scrabble: My word-loving family's go-to game at holiday gatherings
Trivial Pursuit: If you're a fan of Jeopardy, this one's for you.

THE FAVORS

Since our menu had Moroccan flavors, I thought it would be fun to pack up little spice jars of the North African spice mix ras el hanout for guests to take home. While exact ingredients differ from seller to seller, most include some combination of cardamom, cloves, cinnamon, chili peppers, coriander, cumin, peppercorns, paprika, fenugreek, and turmeric. Pick up a large bag from a bulk spice distributor (there are loads of online sources), or buy individual whole spices, toast them, and grind up your own signature mix.

MOROCCAN MANDARIN PUNCH

Greet guests at the door with a pitcher of
Moroccan Mandarin Punch, a delicious fruity
concoction with a whisper of exotic orange
blossom. Combine 1 cup pomegranate juice,
¼ cup orgeat syrup, and ½ cup mandarin
vodka in a pitcher. Stir and then divide evenly
among 6 glasses. Top off with Champagne and
garnish with mint leaves, cinnamon sticks, and
whole star anise.

MOROCCAN ROSE TEA

The tradition of teatime isn't reserved for the
Brits! It's customary in Morocco to follow a
meal with palate-cleansing mint tea. I put
a pretty spin on mine by infusing it with
dried rosebuds. An afternoon of flea market
shopping turned up this intricately carved
Moroccan teapot and gilded glasses that
were absolutely perfect for our after-dinner
tea service. To make, add 1 tablespoon loose
green tea to the teapot and cover with 4 cups
of boiling water. Let it steep for 2 minutes and
then stir in honey to taste and mint sprigs or
rosebuds and let steep 3 to 4 more minutes.

bottoms up!

MIDDLE EASTERN BEERS

Some of the tastiest—and most interesting-looking—beers are imported from the Middle East, so offer
a few of these unexpected beverage options to complement the exotic menu. Check your local market
to find out what imported beer options they offer, and serve bottles iced down in a large galvanized
bucket and allow guests to help themselves.

POPCORN WITH RAS EL HANOUT

The only downside to a big bowl of popcorn? How quickly it disappears when placed in front of hungry guests . . . so make sure to pop a lot! This recipe couldn't be simpler, but the addition of the Moroccan spice ras el hanout combined with a drizzle of olive oil and sea salt makes it 100 percent addictive.

SERVES 6

3 tablespoons extra-virgin olive oil

2 tablespoons ras el hanout

2 teaspoons sea salt

10 cups freshly popped popcorn, still warm

Pour the oil, ras el hanout, and sea salt over warm popcorn. Toss to coat.

SOURCES

Food styling: Ann Lowe
Table linens & serving pieces: Serena & Lily
Serving pieces: Anthropologie

MAKE IT EVEN EASIER

Some of my favorite game night memories are from last-minute thrown-together affairs where everyone (including the host) was relaxed and carefree. If the thought of making all the hors d'oeuvres, mixing cocktails, and cleaning up the house is anxiety provoking, adopt a few of these shortcuts that'll have you hosting like a pro without breaking a sweat.

1 | *Stock up on some extra ras el hanout (used in the favors), and sprinkle over just-popped microwave popcorn for an appetizer that's ready in seconds.*

2 | *Instead of making the soup from scratch, purchase high-quality butternut squash or carrot soup from the grocery store, warm it in a pot on the stove, and then dress it up with the yogurt and parsley garnishes. Your guests will never guess that it's not homemade.*

3 | *Simplify the cocktail by mixing equal parts pomegranate juice and Champagne and then garnish each glass with mint and pomegranate seeds. How bad can that be?*

SPICED NUTS WITH CURRANTS AND APRICOTS

Confession: I actually have to hide these in an upper cabinet after they're made, or else I just might accidentally eat them all myself! For all my fellow salty-sweet fans, this recipe will become your go-to for impromptu snacks with cocktails. During the winter, I love to make a big batch and divide among jars to serve as last-minute hostess gifts for all those holiday parties!

MAKES 3 CUPS

¼ cup currants

⅓ cup sugar

½ tablespoon kosher salt

½ tablespoon chili powder

1 teaspoon ground cinnamon

½ teaspoon ground cumin

½ teaspoon cayenne

1 cup raw almonds

¾ cup shelled pistachios

1 large egg

¼ cup pine nuts

Place the currants in a small bowl and cover with hot water. Set aside.

Preheat the oven to 300°F. Coat a parchment-covered baking sheet with cooking spray.

In a large bowl, combine the sugar, salt, chili powder, cinnamon, cumin, and cayenne. Whisk to combine. Add the almonds and pistachios and toss to coat. In a small bowl, whisk the egg with 1 teaspoon water until frothy and then pour over the nuts and toss to combine.

Working quickly, spread out the nuts on the parchment paper and bake for 25 minutes. Remove the baking sheet from the oven, add the pine nuts, and toss the mixture so that it cooks evenly. Bake for another 15 minutes and then drain the currants and add them to the mix. Stir and return to the oven for 5 to 10 more minutes, until golden brown.

Cool the nuts completely on the baking sheet and then stir at room temperature in an airtight container.

BITS OF BRILLIANCE: *Those twisted knobs of fresh ginger at the market can look a little intimidating if you've never dealt with them before, but with a little know-how, it's a snap to add that spicy sweet kick of ginger to anything you like. (I add it to sweets, savories . . . even my smoothies!) Since chunks of raw ginger are tough and fibrous, I've found grating to be the route that smoothly imparts the most flavor. To do it, use a small spoon to scrape the skin off a piece of ginger, then use firm pressure and a Microplane grater to shower fresh ginger essence right into whatever you're cooking up!*

CARROT SOUP WITH CUMIN AND GINGER

On a buffet of snack food, it's nice to have something that feels a little more substantial, and this warming spicy carrot soup qualifies as total winter comfort food. The sweetness of the carrots combined with the kick of ginger is a much better cure for the common cold than chicken noodle anything, if you ask me. For a gathering like this, I'll serve appetizer-size portions in small bowls or demitasse cups.

MAKES 8 MINI (8-OUNCE) SERVINGS

1 tablespoon butter

1 tablespoon olive oil

1 cup chopped onion

2 tablespoons grated ginger

1 tablespoon minced garlic

1 tablespoon ground cumin

1 tablespoon honey

½ pound carrots, chopped

3 cups chicken broth

1 teaspoon salt

½ cup half-and-half

Plain yogurt, whisked to loosen

Chopped flat-leaf parsley

In a large pot, melt the butter with the olive oil over medium heat. Add the onion and sauté for 4 minutes, until barely translucent. Add the ginger and garlic and cook for 1 minute, stirring constantly. Add the cumin, honey, and carrots and cook for 7 to 8 minutes, until the carrots start to soften. Add the broth and salt and bring to a boil and then reduce the heat to a simmer. Partially cover and cook until the carrots are very tender, about 20 minutes.

Working in batches, transfer the soup to a blender and puree (be careful blending hot ingredients!). Return to the pot and taste to see if more salt is needed. Stir in the half-and-half.

Serve the soup in demitasse cups or small bowls and garnish with a drizzle of yogurt and a sprinkle of parsley.

TANDOORI CHICKEN SKEWERS WITH YOGURT-HARISSA DIPPING SAUCE

Though chicken has a bit of a boring reputation, it's far from dull after hanging out in this lemony yogurt marinade for a couple of hours! Here the chicken is skewered to eliminate the need for a knife and fork during game time, but you could just as easily use the marinade to prep chicken breasts or thighs before tossing them on the grill. Store any extra dipping sauce in the fridge and toss with chopped veggies for a great salad the next day.

MARINADE

Juice of 2 lemons

1 cup whole Greek yogurt

1 tablespoon curry powder

2 garlic cloves, minced

1 tablespoon grated peeled fresh ginger

CHICKEN

1 pound boneless, skinless chicken breasts, patted dry and cut into 1½-inch chunks

4 lemons, thinly sliced into circles

2 tablespoons chopped fresh cilantro leaves, for garnish

YOGURT-HARISSA DIPPING SAUCE

⅔ cup plain whole Greek yogurt

1 teaspoon jarred harissa sauce

1 garlic clove, minced

Juice of 1 lemon

1 tablespoon extra-virgin olive oil

Coarse sea salt

Special equipment: twelve 6-inch wooden skewers

Soak the skewers in water for at least 30 minutes.

To make the marinade, in a small bowl, whisk together the lemon juice, yogurt, curry powder, garlic, and ginger. Set aside.

Drain the skewers and thread 3 or 4 pieces of chicken onto each one, alternating with a lemon slice threaded between pieces.

Place the skewers in a large glass baking dish and use a pastry brush to thoroughly baste the chicken with the marinade. Turn the skewers a few times to coat and then cover with plastic wrap and refrigerate for 1 to 3 hours.

Meanwhile, make the dipping sauce by whisking all the ingredients in a small bowl. Cover and refrigerate until ready to use.

Preheat the grill to medium-high. Remove the skewers from the baking dish and discard the marinade. Cook, turning once, until charred and cooked through, about 4 minutes per side. Garnish with cilantro and serve with the dipping sauce.

19

HOLIDAY
COOKIE SWAP

Every December, my dear friend Myra throws an all-girls cookie swap (with strict instructions to leave the kids and husbands at home!), and we all gather at her house for an afternoon of great company, glasses of bubbly, and of course, way too many sweets! It's a tradition that all her guests have come to look forward to each holiday season, and this year I decided to host my own sugar-fueled version.

Here's the way my cookie swap works: Each guest brings a big batch of her favorite homemade holiday cookies with recipe cards to pass around, and at the party everyone is given a "to go" box in which they collect a sampling of everyone else's signature treats. After a couple hours of mixing and mingling, the ladies leave with a box of two dozen or so different kinds of cookies to sample and (if they're feeling generous) share with family and friends! It's a delicious, and slightly dangerous, way to kick off the holidays, and guests are guaranteed to discover a few new recipes that are destined to become family traditions.

Camille

The MENU

HOLIDAY COOKIE SWAP

This party is all about indulging: taste-testing lots of different cookies and saving healthy-eating resolutions for the new year! Before everyone showed up, I set up a cookie buffet with a few of *my* family's favorite cookies and then let guests add to the mix as they arrived with their creations. To temper a little of that sweetness and provide something more substantial for hungry guests, I set out a big wooden board with cheese and accompaniments. One of the great things about a display like this is that it can be completely prepared and set out before the party, allowing me to be hands-off and sip Prosecco with my girlfriends!

TO DRINK	SAVORY SNACKS	ON THE COOKIE BUFFET
PROSECCO WITH SUGARED CRANBERRIES, PAGE 150	ASSORTMENT OF CHEESES: TRIPLE-CRÈME BRIE, STILTON, AGED CHEDDAR	CHOCOLATE-DIPPED CHERRY ALMOND BISCOTTI, PAGE 153
HOT COCOA WITH PEPPERMINT MARSHMALLOWS, PAGE 150	ORANGE BLOSSOM HONEY, MARCONA ALMONDS, PEARS, CHERRIES	SALTED CHOCOLATE BROWNIE COOKIES, PAGE 154
	FRUITED FLATBREAD, WATER CRACKERS, AND SALAMI	MEXICAN WEDDING COOKIES, PAGE 155
		JAM THUMBPRINT COOKIES, PAGE 158
		CRANBERRY NOELS WITH PISTACHIOS, PAGE 159

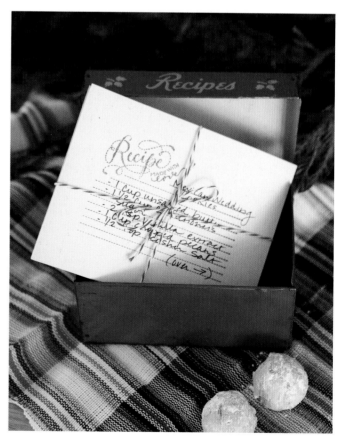

GET THE LOOK

One of my favorite things about having a party around the holidays is that my house is all decked out! The decorated tree, candles flickering on the mantel, and greenery garlands in the entranceway already set the tone for a festive gathering, so all that's left for me to do is set up the cookie buffet and adorn the table with pinecones and evergreen branches.

I approach designing the buffet just as I would any other focal decor element, considering the colors and proportions of the serving pieces and using natural elements to add interest and fullness. When choosing serving pieces, I always look for ways to vary the levels of the different pieces—it gives a balanced feel, and it's much easier for guests to reach the different platters on the table when they're not all at the same height. For this display, I incorporated a beautiful mix of cake stands and tiered pieces—some new and some collected from thrift stores through the years—that literally elevate the cookies to an artistic display.

COPPER AND EVERGREEN

My friend Elizabeth Lewis collects vintage copper vessels—they add an element of warmth that reflects light in such a beautiful way while still feeling timeless and understated. For the simplest, most classic holiday look, we filled one of her copper pitchers with loads of red ilex berry branches and placed it at the center of the cookie buffet. Change the water and snip the bottom of the branches once a week and this arrangement can last all the way through the holiday season!

When creating a vignette with flowers and natural elements, think in terms of threes for the most pleasing arrangement. We combined a single-stem peony and a cluster of festival bush branches in an aged copper vessel and a little grouping of pinecones that filled in any gaps. To finish the look, we laid down a runner made from cedar branches interspersed with pine.

SPICE IT UP

Around the holidays, making craft projects seems especially in keeping with the sentimentality of the season. Handmade items—whether gifted to a friend or kept to display in the home—carry a wonderfully personal touch that makes them likely to become keepsakes, carefully unpacked year after year. As a nod to the culinary theme of our party, I invited my friends to gather around the coffee table to make simple, beautifully scented ornaments out of different kinds of spices. Cinnamon sticks, star anise, and cloves are shaped into snowflakes using hot glue and ribbon, and glitter and other adornments give them a magical luster. Postparty, they're perfect for tying onto holiday packages and, of course, hanging on the tree.

PACKING IT ALL UP

It's crucial that your guests have the right-size vessel for toting home all their cookies . . . and it's nice if it's cuter than a zip-top Baggie! I love to collect vintage Christmas tins at antiques stores throughout the year; they make a really special party favor that guests can use to pack up all their cookies. You can also find sturdy cardboard "to go" boxes at restaurant supply stores—just line them with tissue paper and seal with a sticker or tie with twine. Give guests a couple sheets each of parchment paper to be used as liners between layers, protecting the more delicate cookies.

bottoms up!

PROSECCO WITH SUGARED CRANBERRIES

Create a festive atmosphere with a bubbly bar—Champagne, Prosecco, or cava will do the trick just fine! Set out glasses so guests can help themselves and place skewers of sugared cranberries nearby for the ultimate seasonal stir stick. To make them, boil equal parts sugar and water until the sugar dissolves and then submerge cranberries in the simple syrup. Use a slotted spoon to transfer the cranberries to a cooling rack and let them set for an hour. Roll the cranberries in a shallow bowl filled with sugar to coat and then set aside to dry completely. Once they are dry, thread the sugared cranberries onto wooden skewers for pretty and flavorful stir sticks. These can be made 24 hours in advance and stored in an airtight container in the fridge.

HOT COCOA WITH PEPPERMINT MARSHMALLOWS

At this party, there's no such thing as too much sugar . . . so go ahead and pour a cup of hot cocoa to pair with your cookies! I elevate traditional cocoa with my tried-and-true recipe, plus a few special touches that make it the ultimate. Heat 4 cups whole milk until almost boiling, then add ¼ cup Dutch-processed cocoa, ¼ cup sugar, and 1 to 2 teaspoons vanilla extract. Stir until well dissolved and then pour into 4 mugs and garnish with whipped cream or peppermint marshmallows.

SOURCES

Floral design: The Nouveau Romantics
Food styling: Word of Mouth Catering
Calligraphy: Antiquaria
Props: Loot Vintage Rentals
Tabletop pieces: Anthropologie

A FEW TIPS FOR COOKIE-BAKING SUCCESS

1 | The success of any baking project starts with high-quality ingredients. Good butter (no margarine!), the best chocolate you can afford, and real vanilla extract instead of artificial are musts.

2 | Before beginning, unless otherwise called for, bring all the ingredients (butter, eggs, milk, and so on) to room temperature. This will help the ingredients cream together properly and make a smooth dough.

3 | Unless the recipe specifies otherwise, you'll want to beat sugar and butter together for 3 to 5 minutes, until light and fluffy. But once you add the dry ingredients, turn the mixer to the lowest speed and beat only until everything's combined and the batter is smooth.

4 | Perfect baking relies on accurate measurements of ingredients. When measuring flour, use a spoon to lightly scoop it into the measuring cup to prevent it from packing. Resist the temptation to tap it against the counter or a jar to "settle" the flour; instead, use a knife to gently level off the top. I usually find sifting flour to be an unnecessary and time-consuming step.

5 | Line baking sheets with parchment paper for nonstick cooking and easy cleanup.

6 | A secret tip that gives my cookies the best texture? Chill the cookie dough before baking. Pop into the fridge for an hour (and up to overnight), pressing plastic wrap directly onto the dough's surface to keep air from drying it out. Chilling it will give your dough a little more rise and will keep it from falling flat in the oven.

7 | Invest in high-quality, heavy baking sheets that promote even cooking. Make sure that they're cool or room temperature—scooping cookie dough onto a warm baking sheet will "melt" it, making your cookies too flat. Better to have a few extra baking sheets to let them cool fully between uses.

8 | Halfway through the recommended baking time, switch the cookie sheets from the lower rack to the upper rack and vice versa, and rotate the sheets from front to back, to ensure even baking.

9 | You'll know that cookies are ready to be removed from the oven when only the edges are golden brown. Allow them to sit on the baking sheet for a couple minutes out of the oven, which will finish their baking and allow them to set. Then transfer them to a cooling rack.

10| Cool cookies on wire cooling racks that will let air circulate on all sides, and be sure to let them cool completely before decorating or storing in an airtight container.

BITS OF BRILLIANCE:
In many recipes, dried fruits and nuts are practically interchangeable, so it's a great opportunity to riff on the recipe and swap in your own creative combinations! Besides the cherries and almonds used in this recipe, cranberries with hazelnuts, apricots with pistachios, and raisins with walnuts are all winning duos. Not only does this let you freely make tweaks based on your family's preference, it's also a great way to use up whatever ingredients happen to be hanging out in your pantry!

CHOCOLATE-DIPPED CHERRY ALMOND BISCOTTI

Biscotti is Italian for "twice cooked," and the unique method of slicing the loaf of hot-out-of-the-oven dough and baking each cookie a second time is what gives these cookies their satisfying crunch. They practically beg to be dipped in a cup of coffee, making the chocolate coating indulgently melty . . . and making me want to bring back the tradition of afternoon teatime.

MAKES 5 DOZEN COOKIES

1½ sticks unsalted butter, at room temperature

1 cup sugar

1 teaspoon kosher salt

1 large egg plus 1 egg yolk

1 teaspoon pure vanilla extract

½ teaspoon almond extract

2½ cups all-purpose flour

¾ cup cornmeal

1 teaspoon baking powder

1 teaspoon baking soda

1 cup dried cherries

1 cup slivered almonds, toasted (see page 47)

12 ounces high-quality bittersweet chocolate

Preheat the oven to 350°F and line 2 baking sheets with parchment paper.

In the bowl of a standing mixer on medium speed, beat together the butter, sugar, salt, egg and egg yolk, vanilla, almond extract, flour, cornmeal, baking powder, and baking soda until well combined. Fold in the cherries and almonds.

With well-floured hands, pat the dough into 3 slightly flattened logs (about 15 × 4 inches each) on one of the prepared baking sheets, leaving a few inches between logs.

Bake until golden and firm, about 25 minutes. Let the logs cool on the sheet for 15 to 20 minutes. Use a large spatula to carefully transfer the logs to a cutting board. Use a serrated knife to cut the logs crosswise into ¾-inch slices.

Arrange the slices faceup on the baking sheets. Bake, rotating the sheets and flipping the biscotti halfway through, until golden and crisp, about 15 minutes.

Transfer to wire racks and let cool completely.

To make the dipping sauce, roughly chop the chocolate and place it in a microwave-safe bowl. Microwave at 50 percent power in 30-second intervals, stirring between each one, until the chocolate is smoothly melted.

One at a time, dip the biscotti in chocolate to coat the bottom third of each cookie. Use the rim of the bowl to scrape excess chocolate from each cookie, then return them to the cooling rack and let the chocolate set.

When completely cool, transfer to an airtight container and store at room temperature for up to 1 week.

SALTED CHOCOLATE BROWNIE COOKIES

My husband, Adam, is a huge chocolate lover, and since these include a double dose (melted bittersweet in the dough, mini–chocolate chips folded in at the end), they're pretty much his idea of heaven. The eggs and sugar get beaten together for a surprisingly long time, rendering them light, airy, almost like a soufflé. The addition of crunchy sea salt at the end takes these over the top.

MAKES 20 COOKIES

2 large eggs, at room temperature, lightly beaten

⅓ cup sugar

1 tablespoon brewed espresso

1 teaspoon pure vanilla extract

2 tablespoons (¼ stick) butter

8 ounces bittersweet chocolate, chopped

¼ cup all-purpose flour

¼ teaspoon baking powder

½ teaspoon kosher salt

¾ cup mini–chocolate chips

Maldon sea salt, for finishing

Preheat the oven to 375°F and line 2 baking sheets with parchment paper.

In the bowl of a standing mixer, beat the eggs, sugar, espresso, and vanilla on high speed until thick, 10 to 15 minutes.

Place the butter and bittersweet chocolate in a microwave-safe bowl. Microwave at 50 percent power in 30-second intervals, stirring between each one, until the chocolate is smoothly melted.

Fold the chocolate mixture into the egg mixture until partially combined, leaving some streaks.

In a small bowl, whisk together the flour, baking powder, and kosher salt. Carefully fold the flour mixture into the batter, followed by the chocolate chips. Do not overmix.

Spoon the batter by heaping tablespoons onto the baking sheets. Sprinkle a liberal dose of coarse sea salt on top of each and bake until the cookies are puffy and the tops are cracked, about 9 minutes. Cool before removing from the baking sheets.

MEXICAN WEDDING COOKIES

Mexican wedding cookies have many names: Russian teacakes, snowdrops, and pecan butterballs, to name a few. My grandmother called them sand tarts, and our Christmas Eve growing up was never complete without a big batch of her pecan-studded version. Their buttery flavor recalls traditional shortbread, but these cookies have the added fun of getting whoever eats them covered in powdered sugar. Probably the closest we'll get to a white Christmas here in Austin!

MAKES 4 DOZEN COOKIES

½ pound (2 sticks) unsalted butter, at room temperature

1½ cups confectioners' sugar, sifted

2 teaspoons pure vanilla extract

2 cups all-purpose flour

1 cup finely chopped pecans

½ teaspoon kosher salt

Preheat the oven to 350°F and line 2 baking sheets with parchment paper.

In the bowl of a standing mixer on medium-high speed, beat the butter with ½ cup of the confectioners' sugar until light and fluffy. Add the vanilla and beat to combine. With the mixer on low, gradually add the flour, pecans, and salt until the dough comes together.

Scoop out the dough by the tablespoonful and use your hands to roll it into balls. Place the balls 1 inch apart on the prepared baking sheets.

Bake for 15 minutes, watching closely, until cookies are set but before they begin to turn brown. Immediately transfer the cookies to a wire rack and let cool for 10 minutes.

Place the remaining powdered sugar in a shallow dish. Roll the warm cookies in sugar to coat, then return them to the rack to cool completely.

Once cool, roll the cookies in confectioners' sugar once again. Store them in an airtight container.

JAM THUMBPRINT COOKIES

These are a holiday classic at our house, and I love that the flavors can be changed up depending on your mood. I've filled them with all kinds of jam, honey, and nut butters, swapped out the almond extract for orange or peppermint, and even drizzled the tops with a sugary glaze. It's a great one to get kids involved in, since their little thumbs are perfect for stamping the dough.

MAKES 3 DOZEN COOKIES

1½ cups all-purpose flour

1½ cups slivered almonds, toasted (see page 47)

1 teaspoon baking powder

½ teaspoon kosher salt

½ pound (2 sticks) unsalted butter, at room temperature

½ cup granulated sugar

1 large egg, at room temperature

½ teaspoon pure vanilla extract

½ teaspoon almond extract

½ cup raw sugar

½ cup raspberry jam

½ cup apricot jam

Preheat the oven to 375°F and line 2 baking sheets with parchment paper.

In a food processor, pulse the flour with the almonds until finely ground. Add the baking powder and salt, and pulse to blend.

In the bowl of a standing mixer, beat the butter and sugar until light and fluffy. Add the egg, the vanilla, and the almond extract and beat for 1 minute, or until well combined. Add the dry mixture and mix on the slowest setting until just combined. Refrigerate the dough for 30 minutes.

Place the raw sugar on a plate. Scoop out 1 tablespoon of dough at a time and use your hands to roll into a ball. Roll each ball in sugar, pressing gently to adhere. Place the dough balls a couple inches apart on the prepared baking sheets and then use your thumb to make a deep indentation into each dough ball.

Bake the cookies until golden, about 12 minutes. Halfway through, rotate the baking sheets so the cookies bake evenly. Let the cookies cool for a minute on the pans and then transfer them to wire racks to cool completely.

Use a small spoon to fill half the cookies with raspberry jam and the other half with apricot jam. Store at room temperature in an airtight container for up to 3 days, or freeze the unfilled cookies in a zip-top freezer bag for up to 1 month.

CRANBERRY NOELS WITH PISTACHIOS

I love to keep this dough in my freezer throughout the holiday season so I always feel prepared for impromptu guests (and my own cookie cravings!). To make these in advance, wrap the dough logs tightly in plastic wrap and store in the freezer for up to two weeks. When ready to bake, set out the dough at room temperature until it begins to soften and then slice into disks and proceed with baking.

MAKES 3 DOZEN COOKIES

½ pound (2 sticks) unsalted butter, at room temperature

¾ cup granulated sugar

2 tablespoons whole milk

1 teaspoon pure vanilla extract

2½ cups all-purpose flour

1 teaspoon kosher salt

¾ cup dried cranberries

¾ cup shelled pistachios, chopped

½ cup sparkling sanding sugar

In the bowl of a standing mixer on medium speed, beat the butter and granulated sugar until light and fluffy. Add the milk and vanilla and beat until well combined.

Turn the mixer to the lowest setting and gradually add the flour, then the salt, mixing just until combined. Add the cranberries and chopped pistachios and beat on low until incorporated.

Turn the dough out onto a clean, cool work surface and divide it in half. Form each piece of dough into a round log that's about 2 inches across. Wrap each log in plastic wrap and refrigerate for at least 2 hours, or overnight.

When ready to bake, preheat the oven to 375°F and line 2 baking sheets with parchment paper. Use a sharp knife to cut each log into ¼-inch slices. (Alternatively, form dough into flat disks before placing into freezer, then roll out ⅛-inch thick and cut with holiday cookie cutters.) Place the sanding sugar in a shallow plate and roll edges of each slice in the sugar, lightly pressing to adhere. (If making cutout cookies, sprinkle each with sanding sugar.) Transfer to the prepared baking sheets, leaving at least 1 inch between each cookie.

Bake for 15 minutes, rotating the sheets halfway through, until the cookies start to turn golden on the edges. Transfer the cookies to a wire rack to cool completely.

spring

THE ULTRA-FEMININE FIFTIES

ROSA indica fragrans

CABBAGE
Copenhagen Market
Brassica oleracea

$1.69
1.5 grams

COOL SEASON
95–110 DAYS
Sow in
early spring
or summer

HEIRLOOM
Old-fashioned
favorite.
Compact heads
are sweet for
fabulous
coleslaw, salad
or sauerkraut.
Easy to grow.

Botanical
INTERESTS®

COOL SEASON
180–240 DAYS
Sow in early
spring
(cold climates)
or early fall
(mild climates)

HEIRLOOM
Start indoors
very early for
success in any
climate! Two
mouth-watering
varieties, great
cut flowers
too!

Botanical
INTERESTS®

BOK CHOY
Toy Choy
Brassica rapa (Chinensis group, hybrid)

$2.39
200 mg

COOL SEASON
30–35 DAYS
Sow in
early spring or
late summer

All the flavor
and crispness
of standard
varieties in
a small
package.
A beautiful
single serving
presentation.

Botanical
INTERESTS®

Mr. Dickie Greenleaf
and Ms. Marge Sherwood
Via Roma 57
I–46032 Torino (TO)
Italy

20

>>>>>>>>> EMBRACING THE SEASON <<<<<<<<<

SIGHTS, SOUNDS, AND TASTES OF SPRING

It's called a "spring in your step" for good reason: the most energizing feeling in the world comes from walking outdoors on those first few days of spring, dazzling beams of sunshine warming my spirit and instantly making the gray days of winter a distant memory. My favorite way to spend a springtime afternoon is with my daughter, Phoebe, at the park, high-pitched giggles erupting as I push her higher and higher in the swing. We might pack a simple picnic of sandwiches, some yummy cheese, and fresh berries so we can linger in the grass for as long as possible. When we *are* indoors, this is the season when I long for ways to bring the outdoors into our surroundings, incorporating natural elements into decor and entertaining. One of my favorite days of the year is when the cherryblossom branches arrive at my neighborhood flower market: I gather bunches and group them into an oversize glass jug to place in the center of my dining table. It's the most dramatic centerpiece I have on my table all year and, fortunately, it's also the simplest to create—no floral design skills required!

I've always loved the ritual of spring cleaning: organizing closets, donating items that I don't use or need anymore, and doing those tasks that tend to fall to the bottom of my to-do list during the rest of the year (dusting the baseboards, anyone?). A clean and organized environment never fails to inspire me to freshen up my surroundings with a handful of seasonal touches that reflect the new lightness of my mental state.

Camille

HERE'S HOW I CONNECT WITH ALL THE SENSES TO USHER IN THE SPRING SEASON:

TEXTURE.

Pack away the heavy duvet in the bedroom in favor of a lighter quilt or blanket that's just warm enough to feel cozy on chilly spring nights. Roll up heavy rugs and embrace the coolness of bare floors, or replace them with natural textured rugs like jute or sisal. Consider topping a wool or leather couch with a crisp cotton slipcover in a lighter shade—if it gets dirty, a spin in the washing machine is all that's needed. Although lightness is key, incorporate textural contrast to keep things interesting: sheer lacy table runners look even more delicate when paired with heavier linen napkins.

SCENT.

For the ultimate luxury, I make a lavender linen spray that I use to spritz sheets right out of the dryer, and I'll even put a few drops in the iron so that freshly pressed clothes smell wonderful. To make your own, fill an empty spray bottle with 3 cups of water, ¼ cup vodka, and 1 teaspoon lavender essential oil. Shake well and spray your way to a springtime state of mind! (I'm a major fan of anything that has the potential to make doing laundry more fun!)

COLOR.

For me, it's all about letting in the light and bathing your home in the glow of sunny days; think in terms of white, bright, and airy. I push aside the heavy linen curtains so that sunlight can filter in through gauzy white sheers. In the living room, I create a neutral canvas that allows layers of texture to take on a new dimension. Layering white pillows in different weaves on my nubby taupe couch and accessorizing with natural woven baskets keeps the entire room feeling serene—a haven from the outside world. Even in the most neutral space, I *do* love to add brilliant color with indoor plants. There's no quicker (or more cost-effective) way to add life to a room, and placing a potted fern next to a sunny window brings a welcome shot of green and an organic freshness to the environment.

TASTE.

You know that feeling of biting into the first ripe strawberry of the season? There's no doubt you've made it through a long winter of ho-hum produce when farmers' markets are suddenly bursting with color and freshness! I throw peas, asparagus, and artichoke hearts into spring pasta dishes and frittatas, serve shortcakes piled high with sweetened berries, and garnish cocktails with the fresh mint that's starting to go wild in my herb garden. Now's the time to let vegetables be the star of the show: although we do eat all kinds of fish and meat at our house, I truly believe that when prepared with care and creativity vegetables can be even more interesting than any burger or slab of meat. If you're feeding a carnivore who doesn't consider it a meal unless meat is involved, try making a stir-fry that's primarily made of beautiful vegetables and high-impact seasonings, and throw in just the tiniest bit of chicken. Or try changing up the ratio in a Bolognese sauce so that sautéed onions, carrots, tomatoes, and mushrooms make up most of the texture, with ground beef or bison playing only a small part (instead of the leading role). Of course, cooking this way requires high-quality olive oil; lots of fresh herbs; interesting spices like curry powder and cinnamon; and always a squeeze of something acidic, such as lemon juice or some type of vinegar.

21

SETTING THE SPRING TABLE

I'm always *more* than ready to pack away winter's coats and cozy scarves when the warmer months arrive, and that feeling of shedding extra layers extends to my decor sensibilities as well. When I'm setting the table for springtime dinners, I envision creating a breath of fresh air to the senses—a feeling of lightness in every element. Heavier tablecloths get stashed away for next year's holiday season, and out come vintage lace runners, breezy linen napkins in floral prints, and delicate white plates. For this season's table inspiration, I incorporated found items from nature to bring the outdoors inside for a brunch or dinner gathering, even if the weather's still a bit too chilly for alfresco feasting.

Camille

PALETTE.

Pistachio green, linen, bright white, twig.

LINENS.

A light and earthy striped linen tablecloth is a permanent fixture on my spring table, and I love to top it with slightly thicker nubby linen napkins and delicate glassware. Incorporating as many varied textures as possible provides warmth and interest to a mostly neutral color palette.

CENTERPIECE.

A recycled glass jar filled with gardenias is one of spring's greatest delights! On my wedding day, I tucked a gardenia blossom into my hair, and I still feel flutterings of romance when I catch a whiff of their intoxicating scent. Since gardenias boast the prettiest glossy green foliage, I always incorporate some of the leaves into an arrangement. Gather a few long cuttings and arrange them at different angles, keeping the stems about one and a half times the height of the vessel for a natural look that shows off the organic shape of the flowers.

PLACE SETTINGS.

I fell in love with these textural stoneware plates made in Portugal the moment I laid eyes on them. Their intricate design and crackled mint glaze makes them feel like forgotten china from another era. I paired them with vintage silverware, my everyday linen napkins, and delicate Champagne flutes etched with ethereal floral patterns.

THE DETAILS.

Simple place cards with each guest's name are topped with seedpods that bring an organic feel to each setting. Re-create the look by heading into your own backyard to look for acorns or dried pods, or hit up the produce department at the grocery store for interesting items like lychee nuts, figs, or radishes. Think outside the box and look for unexpected elements with appealing visual form: scavenging at its best!

SOURCES

Location: CTC Garden
Floral design: The Nouveau Romantics
Calligraphy: Mia Carameros
Furniture: Loot Vintage Rentals
Tabletop pieces: Anthropologie

22

SIMPLE APPETIZERS

When I'm hosting any kind of get-together, my number one goal is to make my guests feel welcome, comfortable, and of course, well fed. I love to have some kind of delicious bites ready for grazing upon arrival—it instantly elevates even the most casual gathering and shows guests that I put a little extra thought into making them feel taken care of. I'll set out small bowls of olives, roasted peppers, and cured meats for a simple antipasto spread, or a trio of salsas (classic tomato, mango, and roasted corn are my favorites) with tortilla chips to kick off a dinner party with Mexican flavors on the menu. However, delicious predinner snacks do *not* equal complicated hors d'oeuvres. Who has time to add yet another item to their to-do list when preparing dinner, mixing up drinks, and who knows what else are already on the agenda? I'm a major advocate of appetizers that are either assembled of high-quality store-bought ingredients or that can be prepared completely in advance (and bonus points if they fall into both categories!).

Camille

Simply put together one or two of these perfect combos, arrange on your prettiest platter, pop open the Prosecco, and raise a glass to the fact that the tastiest dishes are often the simplest.

Over the years, I've built an arsenal of a few crowd-pleasing appetizers that I can prepare in *literally* five minutes flat, and what's more, I can usually pull them together with ingredients that I always keep in my pantry or refrigerator (see The Party-Ready Pantry on page 109). Who doesn't want to be that unflappable hostess who whips up a couple of tasty snacks whenever surprise guests stop by? When you've put together your own little assortment of signature snacks, that can be you. And want to know a secret? When it comes to appetizers, it's *less about what you're serving and more about how it's presented.* I've amassed a collection of stylish platters and serving bowls in materials ranging from delicate ceramic to rustic wood that fit whatever vibe I'm trying to create, plus lots of patterned napkins, interesting toothpicks, and colorful little "accent" bowls for dipping sauces and discarded olive pits. Even if I'm serving a humble spread of cheese and crackers, I approach it like a stylist by dressing it up with my best serving pieces and arranging it in an aesthetically pleasing way.

So what are these five-minute snacks I serve up? Hands down, the appetizer I make most often is crostini: interesting ingredients that vary with the seasons, piled atop grilled bread drizzled with olive oil. See page 175 for my ten favorite crostini combinations, but keep in mind: the options are truly endless. I also love to serve any combination of the following.

Grilled fava beans still in their pods, drizzled with olive oil and lemon juice, then sprinkled with Maldon sea salt, freshly cracked pepper, and chili flakes

---

Cooked white beans pureed with garlic, lemon juice, olive oil, and parsley, served with toasted pita wedges

---

Small bowls of roasted peppers, olives, and cured meat with baguette slices

---

A wheel of triple-crème Brie topped with apricot chutney and water crackers

---

Chunks of avocado tossed with mango, halved cherry tomatoes, minced jalapeño, cilantro, and lime juice, served with bell pepper slices and tortilla chips

---

Aged blue cheese (I love Cambozola) with honey, pear slices, and Marcona almonds

---

Fresh radishes with their green tops, high-quality butter, toasted baguettes, and fleur de sel—a classic combination

---

Store-bought tartlet shells filled with creamy goat cheese, roasted figs, and caramelized walnuts

---

Air-popped popcorn drizzled with truffle oil, freshly grated Parmesan, sea salt, and cracked pepper

---

Roasted beets, sliced and drizzled with orange juice, orange zest, and honey, served with a dollop of Greek yogurt

TEN GREAT CROSTINI RECIPES

There's no better five-minute appetizer than crostini—really just a fancy way of saying grilled bread topped with yummy ingredients! I change up the flavor combos based on what's in season (and what happens to be in my fridge), and the ten favorite topping combinations here are really only suggestions. Read over the list to get your creative juices flowing, but feel free to change and adapt based on whatever your taste buds are craving. It all starts with a foolproof foundation: rustic bread that's lightly charred and infused with garlic and olive oil.

Camille

There's no better five-minute appetizer than crostini.

PERFECT CROSTINI

1 loaf rustic country bread or French baguette
(avoid bread that has too many holes in it—the
toppings will fall out too easily)

Extra-virgin olive oil

1 garlic clove

Maldon sea salt or fleur de sel

Heat a grill to high heat (or use a grill pan on
the stove). Slice the bread thinly (½ inch thick or
less) on the bias. Brush both sides of the bread
slices with the oil and then grill until lightly
charred, about 1 minute per side.

Cut the garlic clove in half and rub a cut side
on one side of each grilled bread slice. Sprinkle
lightly with salt and proceed with your toppings
of choice.

MY TEN FAVORITE CROSTINI TOPPINGS

1.

Lemony Avocado. *Thinly sliced ripe avocado topped with crushed red pepper flakes, lemon zest, torn fresh mint leaves, and a sprinkle of sea salt.*

2.

Zucchini and Mint. *Shave raw zucchini into ribbons with a vegetable peeler and top with chopped Marcona almonds, thick shavings of Parmigiano-Reggiano, and torn mint leaves; finish with lemon juice and extra-virgin olive oil.*

3.

Cambozola and Fig. *Top a smear of Cambozola cheese with sliced ripe figs, chopped pistachios, and a drizzle of reduced balsamic vinegar (see page 111).*

4.

Pepper and Olive. *Spread a thin layer of olive tapenade on toast, layer on sliced roasted bell pepper, and top with a sprinkle of toasted pine nuts.*

5.

Peach and Prosciutto. *Lightly grill peach slices when you grill the bread and top the toast with fresh ricotta, thinly sliced prosciutto, the peaches, and a drizzle of honey.*

6.

White Bean and Radish. *Mash cooked white beans with minced garlic, olive oil, and lemon juice; top with sliced radishes, chopped parsley, sea salt, and freshly ground black pepper.*

7.

Goat Cheese and Cherry.
Marinate pitted cherries in port wine and sugar for a couple of hours until they get sweet and syrupy. Top toast with a smear of creamy French goat cheese, macerated port wine cherries, and toasted walnuts (see page 47).

8.

"Cecca" Sauce. *Chop ripe tomatoes and marinate them in garlic, basil, olive oil, and sea salt. Spoon over toast and garnish with chopped scallions and a drizzle of truffle oil.*

9.

Pesto and Portobello. *Spread a thin layer of pesto on toast and top with slices of roasted portobello mushroom, thinly sliced mozzarella, and a few fresh arugula leaves.*

10.

BLT. *Chopped tomatoes, crumbled crispy bacon, arugula, and a drizzle of garlic oil.*

24

LIVING WITH SPRING FLOWERS

The first hint of spring's arrival is usually my cue to head to the nearest flower market and pick up an armful of flowering branches. Quince, dogwood, cherry blossom—all of them make me swoon! Just as the advent of spring speaks to change and newness, the fleeting nature of flowers is a fresh reminder to embrace the present moment and surround ourselves with beauty.

An oversize jar filled with branches on my dining table or a bud vase bearing delicate peonies in the bathroom is a quick way to transform my home for the season, and the warmer temperatures present the perfect opportunity to head into the great outdoors for a bit of foraging. Each time I walk outside and truly engage my senses, I'm thrilled by the potential to create something beautiful with what's right in front of my eyes. A pruned branch from the olive trees in my backyard, pods I uncover in the woods behind my house, and even a few leaves of kale from my vegetable garden are all fair game for experimentation.

An added bonus to the flowers that bloom at this time of year? Many of them carry an intoxicating scent that fills the house with the fragrance of the season. Trailing jasmine, frilly stock, and vibrant daffodils all yield a scent that elicits total spring fever.

Camille

BITS OF BRILLIANCE:
If peonies are closed when you buy them and you'd like to open up their blooms a bit, place the stem in warm water to make them open faster. If you're working with really tight buds, put the head of the flower in warm water for a couple of minutes, then place the stem in water to see a significant "pop."

NO. 1

SINGLE-STEM PEONIES

Is it any wonder that peonies seem to be the most photographed flower in the blogosphere? I've always been a bit obsessed—so much so that I actually scheduled my wedding for late spring, when peonies are at their prettiest. My bridal bouquet was a loose bunch of white petals and trailing vines, and the palest blush pink peonies dotted every table at our reception. My personal heaven.

Nothing makes you feel more pampered than waking up to peonies on your dressing table, so Elizabeth designed the simplest grouping of single-stem bud vases that are the most entry-level design—ideal for someone with zero floral-arranging experience.

CHOOSE THE VESSELS.

When arranging a group of single stems, use bud vases in similar materials (for example, different shades of green glass) or different materials that are tied together in a similar color palette (such as ceramic and glass vases in all white). And don't forget to think beyond the vase! Stemless wineglasses or small water glasses are some of the best vessels for holding single stems. The important thing to look for is a small opening that will hold the flower in place.

CHOOSE THE FLOWERS.

We prefer large single blooms placed in bud vases; lots of little flowers bunched together can result in a "squeezed" appearance. If you do want to incorporate smaller delicate flowers, try using three stems per vase (long and leggy flowers like ranunculus or sweet peas are perfect) cut to three different heights.

PUT IT TOGETHER.

When arranging peonies, cut off each leaf section and then pair one leafy stem with each flower. Use the same variety of peonies for a lush, monochromatic look, or mix them up for a subtle yet gorgeous variation in shades, as we did here. Embrace the simplicity of this arrangement—don't overthink it!—and group en masse. Go with odd numbers: one, three, or five bud vases together.

A beautiful thing about bringing peonies into the home is that their color will change and fade as they age. I love the fresh beauty of tighter buds and leafy greens, yet fully open peonies in their final stages of life, with most of the color faded out and petals beginning to drift to the floor, are equally intoxicating.

NO. 2

BLOOMING BRANCHES

I've written earlier in the book about my love for blooming branches, but it's worth repeating that there's no simpler way to bring seasonality and drama onto the dining table. Have you ever noticed how often branches grace the pages of interior design magazines? Decorators love them as much as I do, both for their organic sculptural quality and their ability to provide major bang for the buck. For this arrangement, Elizabeth gathered a big bunch of snowy-white spirea in an oversize recycled glass jar. They're undeniably evocative of the season, but I must admit that I'd love to have them on my table all year long!

CHOOSE THE VESSEL.

Branches are best kept long to fully show off their beautiful organic shape, so use a tall or widemouthed vase, jar, bottle, or pitcher.

CHOOSE THE BRANCHES.

My flower market carries a variety of flowering branches in the spring, but this is really the perfect time to grab your clippers and do some foraging on a nature walk. Just make sure to ask permission from your neighbors before you start "pruning" their trees!

PUT IT TOGETHER.

Thick branches should be cut on an angle: the goal is to increase the surface area of the part of the branch that can absorb water. You can also use your hands to break off the bottom of the branch and then pull it apart at the bottom so that water can easily flow into the branch. Cluster a mass of a single variety of branches together—we used spirea—for a pretty and simple arrangement that can last for weeks, depending on the variety.

NO. 3

DELICATE GARDEN BLOOMS

The bedside table is such a personal space: the first thing I lay eyes on when I wake up in the morning and the last thing I see when I turn off the light. I make an effort to keep it clean, uncluttered, and a bit luxurious, with a small cluster of fresh flowers and a wonderfully scented candle that I love to burn while I read in bed. Since this space calls for something petite and contained, it's a perfect opportunity to use pretty, delicate flowers that will make me smile when my alarm goes off each morning (priceless!). For this arrangement, we chose a variety of graceful blooms: astrantia, sweet peas, geraniums, forget-me-nots, grape hyacinth, and anemones.

CHOOSE THE VESSEL.

Our vase had a wider mouth, so we filled it with a generous amount of spring flowers for a lush feel. Since the bedside table is a small space, you could easily get away with using fewer flowers—just make sure to match them with a vase that has a narrower mouth.

CHOOSE THE FLOWERS.

To highlight the gradient of colors in this arrangement, we started with the dappled purple sweet peas, which bridged the bold blue grape hyacinth with the more sculptural white anemones. The result is a beautiful ombré effect that feels at once vivid and serene. If you love monochromatic arrangements the way I do, think about riffing off that look by using a gentle mix of varying hues: a spectrum of pinks, a gradient of creams, or a cluster of blues that mimics the transition when sea fades into sky.

PUT IT TOGETHER.

When using a wider-mouthed vase, start the arrangement with stems that have offshoots (multiple stems coming off one branch). We used geranium and astrantia leaves to create a "basket" of interwoven stems and then fed the more delicate sweet peas through the crisscrossed stems to hold them steady. This created a sturdy base into which the *most* delicate stems—in this case, grape hyacinth and anemones—could be added exactly where we wanted them, held in place by the structure we'd created.

NO. 4

ELEGANT TULIPS AND WISPY VINES

My favorite arrangements combine an architectural shape with a haphazard element, and this grouping of curving, curling clematis vines with arching tulips does both perfectly. Elizabeth created it for a side table in a cozy reading nook, breathing color and springtime energy into an otherwise neutral spot. Whenever I lay eyes on these utterly captivating fringed tulips in the flower market, I just *have* to scoop them up: their ruffly texture adds an unmistakably feminine quality to any bouquet.

CHOOSE THE VESSEL.

Since both tulips and clematis have long stems that are prone to drooping, they work best in a vessel that has a narrow mouth opening to provide support. However, it's also best to choose something with height, so that once the stems start to fold over into their graceful droop, a tall vessel can provide a sense of balance.

CHOOSE THE FLOWERS.

Choose tulips that aren't too open if you'd like them to last several days—I love to watch their shape change and unfold. Tulips continue to grow toward the light even after they're cut, so embrace the fact that they *will* droop and fall over. The resulting look is so moody and romantic!

PUT IT TOGETHER.

This arrangement is meant to be organic, light, and airy, and using a minimal number of flowers allows the flowers to breathe. Group like colors together (dark purples, violets, and whites) and create a sense of "balanced asymmetry" by keeping the arrangement tighter on one side and looser on the other. Clematis are one of the few flowers that don't like flower food, so just fill the vase with clean water each day and trim ½ inch off the bottom of the stems each time to encourage water absorption. And don't forget that clematis are toxic flowers, so be sure to keep them out of reach of children and pets!

BEYOND THE VASE

I doubt I'm the only one with a linen closet full of vases of just about every possible shape and size; some were purchased on a whim, while others came with a florist delivery and then got stashed away to collect dust. As I've developed more of a signature floral style and experimented with using different vessels, more often than not I find myself reaching for something that's not even a vase in the traditional sense: a silver pitcher I found at an antiques shop, my favorite handmade pottery mug, and an empty glass bottle that once held French hand soap are some of my current favorite ways to display cut flowers.

When I'm choosing the vessel for an arrangement, I consider the proportions, colors, and overall vibe of the flowers that will go in it. Wildflowers look pretty and effortless in vintage bottles; composed groupings appear elegant in a compote dish with vines trailing over the sides. We chose vases with narrow openings for arrangements made of just a few stems and a wider-mouthed vessel for a lush look using lots of blooms.

25

THE FIVE-MINUTE BEAUTY FRESHEN-UP

We've all been there. You're rushing to put the finishing touches on dinner for a crowd, tidying up the living room, and turning on music when you look at the clock and realize that guests will be showing up at the door in five minutes—barely enough time to change out of that sauce-splattered blouse, let alone attend to your hair and makeup! But since a calm hostess sets the stage for a welcoming atmosphere, taking the time to look (and feel) your best is a crucial step that will help you answer the door with a big smile and warm greeting. And I've discovered that when I'm feeling confident and comfortable in my own skin, it frees me up to focus all my attention on making my guests feel cherished. Since I rarely have time to fully get ready before a party (and I bet you don't, either), I've mastered what I call the five-minute freshen-up: a few quick—and I mean *quick*—touches that will help you feel less like you've been prepping in the kitchen and more like a radiant guest, sparkling at her own party. An added bonus to applying makeup with a light hand? Instead of hiding behind a face full of foundation, your natural beauty can shine through. Here's what I do when the clock is ticking.

Camille

1 | *Use blotting papers or a piece of tissue to lightly dab any oil or excess makeup on your face, creating a smooth canvas. Use fingertips to dab a creamy concealer under eyes and on eyelids, around nostrils, on the chin, and on any blemishes. Then blend, blend, blend.*

2 | *Dab a pinkish cream or gel blush onto the apples of your cheeks for an instant flush.*

3 | *With a fluffy brush, apply loose powder all over your face in a circular motion. I find that a powder with yellow undertones and light-reflecting particles instantly warms up all shades of skin and boosts the "glow" factor.*

4 | *Curl eyelashes with an eyelash curler (nope, can't skip this step!) and then apply a coat of black mascara, wiggling the wand back and forth to completely coat lashes from roots to tips. If you have superlight eyebrows like mine, use a brow pencil that's one shade lighter than your natural color to make tiny strokes, filling in the brow line.*

5 | *If you only have thirty seconds total, skip steps 1 through 4—but don't forget to slick on a bright shade of lipstick and flash those pearly whites!*

TWO MINUTES TO LOVELY LOCKS

The day of a party, I do my best to blow out and style my hair in the morning, since I know I probably won't have time to do it later. But by six o'clock, my fine hair has almost certainly lost its oomph. To revive limp locks, dry shampoo is the secret weapon that—with a few strategic spritzes at the roots—soaks up any greasiness and makes hair full of va-va-volume. There are a few salon brands that smell great, but even cheap drugstore versions do the trick. Flip hair over and use fingers to "mess it up" a bit, then flip back up and use a brush to lightly smooth the top layer of strands. If all else fails, twist your hair up into a chic bun on top of the head or pull it into a low, sleek ponytail for instant sophistication.

26

CREATING A WELCOMING GUEST ROOM

Full disclosure: I love hotels. There's something that feels so luxurious about ordering room service, popping open the heavenly scented complimentary toiletries, and most of all, slipping into those crisp, clean sheets and resting your head on the puffiest down pillow. When we moved into our house a few years ago and I had a designated guest room for the first time, I wanted to create an experience for visiting family and friends that felt as close to a hotel getaway as possible. The great thing is, the little touches that create a luxe vibe don't have to be expensive and certainly don't require the skills of an interior designer. It's all about focusing on a few small details that make the space feel stylish and welcoming while ruthlessly editing out any clutter that could detract from the overall feeling of serenity. An added bonus is that your guests will be so comfortable that they'll want to go to bed early and sleep late, letting you ease into the weekend at a slower pace as well. Here are a few ways to make the guest room incredibly inviting.

Camille

LAY THE FOUNDATION.

Start with a good-quality box spring, mattress, and mattress pad. One hundred percent wool mattress pads are hypoallergenic and resist odors, and they provide a welcome layer of cushioning. And don't forget to flip the mattress twice a year to keep it feeling fresh.

DRESS THE BED.

Since people's comfortable sleeping temperatures can vary wildly, think in terms of layers that can be added to or subtracted from the mix. There are loads of options when it comes to selecting the fabric for your fitted and flat sheets; head to a bedding store and feel the differences between Egyptian cotton, percale, satin, and jersey to find your personal preference. If you (like most people) are intimidated by the variety of thread count options, just remember that 200 is good, 300 is great, and anything above 400 provides such an undetectable difference that it's probably not worth the higher price. Don't forget that you'll want to lay the flat sheet on the bed with wrong side up—that way, when you fold the top down over a blanket, the right side will be showing. Next comes a light blanket or quilt, and a heavier blanket or duvet can be folded at the end of the bed for chilly nights.

PILLOW TALK.

Pillows are definitely a matter of preference, so I lay down two flatter pillows first and then take a cue from luxury hotels and top them with the puffiest down-filled pillows I can get my hands on. Guests will want to sink into the bed the minute they lay eyes on them! Two big shams and one chic accent pillow or bolster finish the look; I nix the collection of little decorative pillows that can start to make things look messy (and usually just get thrown on the floor, anyway).

GO GREEN.

There's no easier or more cost-effective way to inject a major dose of style to the guest room than with a couple of well-placed houseplants. A fiddlehead fig tree adds immediate drama to an empty corner and requires little care beyond weekly watering. Small ferns placed on a nightstand or desk provide a feeling of serenity, and succulents add major cool factor and are practically hands-off when it comes to care (perfect for those who, like me, lack a green thumb). In addition to adding beauty, bringing plants into the room actually increases guests' well-being! They increase oxygen levels, remove toxins from the air, and have been shown to decrease fatigue, colds, and headaches. How's that for creating a positive atmosphere?

THE FINAL TOUCHES.

These are the details that make your guest room one for the books, and they're actually the simplest (and most fun) to implement. Create a welcoming aroma by placing a beautiful fig, floral, or linen-scented candle on the nightstand, and don't forget to include a pretty box of matches in the top drawer. Place a carafe of water with a glass nearby, and stack a few recent issues of magazines that would appeal to your guest's individual taste; I leave *Vogue* for out-of-town girlfriends, *Bon Appétit* for my mom, and *Texas Monthly* for my homesick brother. And I always try to place a couple of local Austin magazines that include the best places to eat, go for a hike, and shop—they serve as a mini-travel guide on what's new and happening for out-of-towners! I make sure the bathroom is stocked with any necessary toiletries that my guests may have forgotten: shampoo, conditioner, shower gel, body lotion, toothpaste, and a toothbrush (still in its packaging, please). Stock up on travel-size containers at Target or Sephora (or nab some from the bathroom of a hotel while you're traveling), so you can always treat guests to unused items—remember, we're aiming for the hotel experience here! A bud vase with a couple of pretty blooms and an extra beautiful hand towel placed by the sink are both lovely touches. Hand-woven Turkish towels are one of my favorite splurges, adding an exotic splash of color to an otherwise serene space. Finally, hang a white terry or waffle-weave robe on the back of the door for the ultimate pampering touch. Size large seems to work for most people.

Creating a space that my guests will love is all about extending a spirit of generosity and mindfulness to everyone who stays at my home. It sends a message that I've gone the extra mile to make sure that our time together is unforgettable. Of course, this makes it critical to invite only people I genuinely want to spend time with, because by the time my guests leave, they're often already planning their return trip.

HOSTING OVERNIGHT GUESTS . . . WITHOUT A GUEST ROOM

Until a few years ago, I'd always lived in small spaces without a designated guest room, so I got a lot of practice making guests feel just as comfortable and well cared for in a makeshift guest area. By no means should you let lack of space deprive you of the fun of hosting overnight visitors! Remember that a gracious and welcoming attitude is the most valuable tool in your arsenal, no matter what size house or apartment you're in. Here are a few tips for making "pop up" guest quarters as cushy as possible.

1. *Think about all the options when it comes to bedding. There are really comfortable futons on the market that can double as a living room couch and a guest bed. Even a blow-up mattress placed in a home office can be inviting when dressed with great sheets and a luxurious duvet or blanket.*

2. *Place a carafe of water with a glass, a great-smelling candle, a few flowers in a bud vase, and some current magazines or books next to the bed.*

3. *This one is crucial: clean up the room before guests arrive! The last thing we want is for them to feel like an afterthought . . . which they will if they're surrounded by your stacks of mail and work projects. Clear away any unnecessary clutter, clean up around the bed, remove items from a nearby table so that guests can use it as a nightstand, and provide a closet for them to stash their suitcase and hang up clothes.*

Above all, consider how to send the message to your guests to make themselves 100 percent at home. Let them know where snacks and filtered water are stashed, and make it easy for them to come and go at their leisure. Leave a note that includes some of your favorite spots in town that they might want to visit, and be sure to include any garage or alarm code info they might need in order to return to your house. Setting such a welcoming tone goes further than any lavishly appointed guest room!

27

SPRING CELEBRATION BRUNCH

My daughter, Phoebe, just turned nine months old, and as nature shakes off winter's chill and reveals the early signs of spring, our family is anticipating all kinds of sweet little firsts, too: Phoebe's first Easter (and you can bet that I'm already filling her basket with a few baby treats); her first glimpse of blooming flowers and fruit on our lemon tree; inaugural trips to the park now that warm weather has arrived; and my very first Mother's Day as a mom. There's no doubt that we have some celebrating to do, so I planned a springtime brunch to welcome the season by gathering a few friends for a midday farm-to-table feast. My menu would be perfect for an Easter meal followed by an egg hunt, a Mother's Day brunch, or even a bridal shower for a summer bride!

And there are so many reasons to host a get-together early in the day: little ones can join in on the festivities, and everyone seems to arrive relaxed and unhurried. I prepped several elements of the menu the night before so that I was left with just a few manageable tasks to do the morning of the party. In true celebration of nature's beauty, I headed to a courtyard near my house that's covered in blooming jasmine vines perfuming the air with the fragrance of spring, and I set up a rustic farm table topped with natural linens, bunches of lilacs, and big platters of seasonal food that we passed around the table family-style. Enjoying brunch on a gorgeous day surrounded by some of my very favorite women? Talk about starting spring on the right foot!

Camille

The
MENU
SPRING CELEBRATION BRUNCH

My brunch menu was a hybrid of lunch-y things infused with breakfast flavors, bursting with colorful, zesty fruits and vegetables inspired by the gorgeous produce overflowing farmers' markets at this time of year. As guests arrived, I set out the simplest prebrunch nibbles that Peter Cottontail would have surely approved: a classic combination of French spring radishes paired with baguette, butter, and sea salt and an ice-cold pitcher of fragrant lavender lemonade. Once we'd had a chance to hang out and let the kids run around in the grass for a bit, we all gathered at the farm table that I'd preset with a rustic asparagus and bacon tart, colorful salads, and, to get everyone in a celebratory mood, glasses of crisp Champagne.

TO DRINK	PREBRUNCH NIBBLES ON A SIDE TABLE	BRUNCH, SERVED FAMILY-STYLE
CHAMPAGNE COCKTAILS, PAGE 206 LAVENDER LEMONADE, PAGE 206	FRENCH RADISHES WITH BUTTER, MALDON SEA SALT, AND SLICED BAGUETTE	ROASTED CARROTS WITH TARRAGON BROWN BUTTER, PAGE 208 SHAVED SQUASH SALAD WITH MARCONAS AND FETA, PAGE 209 CLEMENTINE–VANILLA BEAN UPSIDE-DOWN CAKE, PAGE 211 ASPARAGUS, BACON, AND GOAT CHEESE TART, PAGE 213 SUNSHINE GRANOLA, PAGE 215

GET THE LOOK

Vibrant lilac and spring pea green really pop against a clean white canvas. I didn't want to completely cover the raw beauty of a rough-hewn farm table, so I topped it with a neutral runner that left the edges of the table exposed, as well as a few bunches of flowers arranged casually in earthenware containers and food served family-style on big platters perfect for passing. This brunch has a definite garden party vibe—host it in the backyard, in a neighborhood park, or even at a local nursery or botanical garden.

APRIL SHOWERS . . .

There's a reason this season is known for both sunshine and rain—the weather can be extremely unpredictable! Depending on where you live, spring days can be incredibly beautiful or dark and stormy. The moral of the story? When planning *any* kind of outdoor affair, have an alternative indoor location in mind, or plan to reschedule on a future rain date. I learned this lesson the hard way too many times during my years as an event planner: you *cannot* be overly prepared when it comes to dealing with inclement weather.

. . . BRING MAY FLOWERS

My florist friend Elizabeth Lewis was inspired by the memories of springtime gatherings with friends and family—the nostalgic fragrance of lilac perfectly captures the essence of those treasured memories. The additions of clematis's trailing vines and ranunculus's bright, happy blooms marry the best of the season's flowers in an effortlessly beautiful way, especially when arranged simply in ceramic pitchers or garden urns. When picking lilacs from the garden or buying them at the market, choose blooms with most of the florets open, since they stop opening once they've been harvested.

I shall not be likely to go to town while the lilacs bloom.

—Longfellow

HAVE A BALL

This party practically begs for lawn games that appeal to a variety of ages. Before guests arrive, set out the equipment for games of bocce ball, croquet, or horseshoes on the lawn to encourage a little friendly competition. Anything that gets guests out of their seats and interacting instantly makes a party more fun, and a couple of rousing games give everyone extra encouragement to soak up the sunshine long after the last slice of clementine cake is gone.

THE FAVORS

I wanted to send everyone home with a little something sweet, so in keeping with our brunch theme, I packed up jars of my signature Sunshine Granola, which can be enjoyed the next day for breakfast. To make them, I purchased mason jars in different sizes and cut circles out of pretty kraft and patterned papers to fit under the screw-on lid. Using small alphabet stamps (one of the best investments ever for those of us who aren't calligraphers), I labeled each jar and then hot-glued twine around the outer ring of the lid to add a rustic textural element. A similar technique could be used for packing up all sorts of favors besides granola: fresh jam, local honey, or sugar that's been infused with citrus peel would all make lovely parting gifts.

bottoms up!

CHAMPAGNE COCKTAILS

I ardently love a classic Champagne cocktail: it doesn't get much simpler yet adds an undeniable dose of festivity to any celebration. To make, add a sugar cube and a couple drops of bitters to a Champagne flute. Let the bitters soak in and then add a few berries (whatever you like!) and fill the glass to the top with Champagne. There's just something about those first fizzy bubbles tickling my nose that sends an instant message to my brain: it's time to kick back, soak up the sunshine, and revel in the moment.

LAVENDER LEMONADE

I was recently at a party where the host served a lavender-infused lemonade, and I was enchanted from the first sip: springtime flowers in a glass! I was determined to re-create it at home, and this version comes pretty darn close. Start by making a lavender simple syrup: in a medium saucepan, bring 1 cup water, 1 cup sugar, and 2 tablespoons dried lavender flowers to a simmer and let simmer until the sugar is dissolved. Turn off the heat and cool completely. Strain the simple syrup into a large pitcher with 1 cup cold water, 1 cup fresh-squeezed lemon juice, and lots of ice and stir to combine. Set it out in a beverage dispenser or pretty pitcher so your guests can serve themselves when they arrive—such a refreshing start to your garden gathering!

SOURCES

Location: Big Red Sun
Floral design: The Nouveau Romantics
Food styling: Ann Lowe
Furniture: Liv by Design
Table linens & bar cart: Serena & Lily
Tabletop pieces: Anthropologie

BITS OF BRILLIANCE:

I love adding citrus to brighten a dish, and to really intensify the flavors, I'll often add the juice and the zest. I rely on my Microplane grater to finely grate the peel without getting any of the bitter pith and then I cut the fruit in half and squeeze it facedown into my fingers to release the juice while trapping any seeds. The zest-juice double whammy is especially delicious in salad dressings, muffins, and any kind of roasted seasonal vegetables, like these carrots.

ROASTED CARROTS WITH TARRAGON BROWN BUTTER

I love carrots prepared just about any way, but Adam's never been much of a fan . . . that is, until I made these sweet and citrusy ones that even he deemed "totally addictive." I think tarragon is a highly underappreciated herb, and I love the subtle licorice flavor that it adds to this recipe.

SERVES 4

2 bunches young carrots, with tops (if you can find multicolored, they're really pretty in this recipe!)

¼ cup extra-virgin olive oil

Sea salt and freshly ground black pepper

6 tablespoons (¾ stick) unsalted butter

1 tablespoon orange zest

¼ cup orange juice

1 tablespoon brown sugar

1 tablespoon chopped fresh tarragon leaves, plus more for garnish

Preheat the oven to 400°F and line a baking sheet with parchment paper.

Cut off all but 1 inch of the carrot tops. Toss the carrots with the oil and a big pinch of sea salt and a generous grinding of pepper on the prepared baking sheet. Roast for 20 minutes, until fork tender but not mushy.

In the meantime, melt the butter in a small skillet over medium-low heat. Add the orange zest, orange juice, and sugar. Swirl the pan until the butter starts to brown and smells nutty. Stir in the tarragon.

Arrange the carrots on a platter and drizzle with the tarragon brown butter. Garnish with fresh tarragon and serve.

BITS OF BRILLIANCE:

I first experienced Marcona almonds at a wine-tasting party several years ago. After popping one in my mouth, I thought, "What is this taste of heaven that's somewhere between an almond and a hazelnut?" Ever since, they've been a permanent fixture in my freezer—since Marconas have a very high oil content, they spoil quickly when kept in the pantry. Although they're more expensive than your average almond, Marconas elevate every dish to something really special. Try them sprinkled on salads, served on a cheese plate, or devoured as a luxurious midafternoon snack.

SHAVED SQUASH SALAD WITH MARCONAS AND FETA

This is one of my very favorite salad recipes and also one of the simplest. I make it all summer long when summer squash is in its peak of season, which is extra important here, since it's served raw so that you can really taste its fresh flavor. The thin ribbons are so pretty and look a little bit fancy, although they can be made in just a few minutes with any basic vegetable peeler.

SERVES 8

4 zucchini, yellow squash, or any other summer squash

8 cups baby arugula

Leaves from 1 fresh mint stem, finely chopped

1 teaspoon finely grated lemon zest

3 tablespoons lemon juice

⅓ cup extra-virgin olive oil

Sea salt and freshly ground black pepper

½ cup Marcona almonds

½ cup crumbled feta

Using a vegetable peeler, shave the squash in long ribbons into a large salad bowl. When you get to the seeded center of each squash, stop and discard. Add the arugula to the bowl.

In a small bowl, whisk together the mint, lemon zest, and lemon juice. While whisking, slowly stream in the oil. Season to taste with salt and pepper.

Add just enough dressing to the salad to lightly coat the squash and arugula. Toss to combine.

Roughly chop the Marcona almonds and add them and the feta to the bowl, and gently combine. Then season with a bit more sea salt as needed.

CLEMENTINE–VANILLA BEAN UPSIDE-DOWN CAKE

I have two requirements for homemade desserts for a party: they've got to be beautiful, and I must be able to completely prepare them in advance. This cake absolutely fulfills both. The concentric spirals of caramelized clementines make this cake a real stunner—a completely fresh take on the traditional upside-down cakes that were so popular in the 1950s and '60s. Make it the night before the brunch, so all that's left to do is slice it up and top with honey crème fraîche. And brew the coffee, of course.

SERVES 10

TOPPING

5 clementines, thinly sliced (peel intact) and seeds removed

4 tablespoons (½ stick) unsalted butter

¾ cup (packed) light brown sugar

CANDIED CLEMENTINE SLICES (OPTIONAL)

1 cup granulated sugar

4 clementines, thinly sliced and seeds removed

CAKE

1½ cups all-purpose flour

3 tablespoons cornmeal

1½ teaspoons baking powder

1 teaspoon kosher salt

½ cup heavy cream, at room temperature

1 teaspoon clementine zest (from about 2 clementines)

¼ cup freshly squeezed clementine juice (from 1 medium or 2 very small clementines)

2 vanilla beans

8 tablespoons (1 stick) unsalted butter, softened at room temperature

1 cup plus 2 tablespoons granulated sugar

4 large eggs, separated, at room temperature

1 cup crème fraîche

2 tablespoons honey

(continued on the next page)

To make the topping: Bring a large pot of water to a boil. Add the clementine slices and cook for 3 minutes, then use a slotted spoon to remove them to a paper-towel-lined plate. Spread out in a single layer and set aside to dry for 1 hour.

Grease the bottom and sides of a 9-inch round cake pan. In a medium saucepan, melt the butter on low heat. Add the brown sugar and increase the heat to medium. Cook, stirring occasionally, for about 4 minutes, until the caramel lightens in color and gets foamy. Working very quickly, pour the mixture into the prepared cake pan and swirl to coat evenly. Arrange the clementine slices in concentric circles over the topping. Press the fruit lightly into the topping and set aside.

Set an oven rack in the center of the oven and preheat the oven to 350°F.

To make the cake: In a medium bowl, whisk together the flour, cornmeal, baking powder, and salt.

In a small bowl, combine the cream, zest, and juice. Cut the vanilla beans lengthwise, scrape the seeds into the bowl (reserving the pods for another use), and whisk to combine.

In the bowl of a standing mixer, cream the butter on medium-high speed. Very slowly add 1 cup of the granulated sugar and beat for 3 minutes until light and fluffy. Add the egg yolks, one at a time, and beat well, scraping down the sides of the bowl with a rubber spatula when necessary.

Reduce the speed to the lowest setting and add the dry ingredients and cream mixture alternately in 3 batches, beginning and ending with the dry ingredients. Beat just until smooth and then transfer the batter to a very large mixing bowl.

Clean and dry the standing mixer, add the egg whites, and beat them on low speed just until frothy. Increase the speed to medium-high and beat to soft peaks. Gradually add the remaining 2 tablespoons of granulated sugar and continue to beat until stiff peaks form.

Fold a quarter of the beaten egg whites into the batter with a spatula to lighten the mixture. Add the remainder of the whites to the batter and fold until no streaks remain. Carefully pour the batter over the clementines in the pan and spread evenly.

Bake until the top of the cake is golden and a toothpick inserted just into the cake (not the topping) comes out clean, 55 to 60 minutes.

Let the cake rest in the pan for 2 minutes on a wire rack. Run the edge of a paring knife all the way around the sides to dislodge any stuck bits. Place the wire rack over the pan and carefully invert the cake onto the rack. Tap a couple times and then remove the pan. If any fruit is still stuck to the pan, you can remove it and arrange it on top of the cake (no one will ever notice!). Allow the cake to cool completely.

Meanwhile, in a small bowl, beat the crème fraîche with the honey.

If topping with additional candied clementines, bring the granulated sugar and 1 cup water to a simmer in a medium saucepan. Add the clementine slices and let simmer for 20 minutes. Remove with a slotted spoon to a paper-towel-lined plate and set aside to cool. Use to garnish the top of the cake as desired.

Use a serrated knife to cleanly slice through the clementine topping when cutting the cake, and serve slices with the honey crème fraîche.

BITS OF BRILLIANCE:

Blind baking (or prebaking) is a crucial step in this recipe, as it keeps the center of the dough from puffing up too much or becoming soggy. I like to keep a bag of dried beans in my pantry that I use over and over just for blind-baking pie crusts; after I'm done with them, I put them back in their labeled plastic bag and reserve them for the next time I need them!

ASPARAGUS, BACON, AND GOAT CHEESE TART

Although I love to cook, I can definitely be a bit lazy . . . and making homemade piecrust from scratch just doesn't sound like the way I'd like to spend a beautiful spring day. My love of quiche and eggy tarts inspired me to develop this version using store-bought puff pastry, which practically bakes itself . . . and tastes every bit as good as its homemade pastry counterpart. Try to use all-butter puff pastry if possible: there's a world of difference in the flavor compared with the versions made with hydrogenated oils. I filled mine with crispy bacon, seasonal asparagus, and a creamy egg mixture that's totally decadent yet somehow feels light and seasonal at the same time.

SERVES 6

1 sheet all-butter puff pastry from a 14-ounce package (I like the Dufour brand)

4 large eggs

6 tablespoons half-and-half

1 tablespoon chopped fresh thyme

Kosher salt and freshly ground black pepper

4 scallions (white and green parts), sliced on the diagonal

3 tablespoons cream cheese, at room temperature

8 slices bacon, cooked and crumbled

1 4-ounce package crumbled goat cheese

20 thin asparagus spears, trimmed

Maldon sea salt, for finishing (optional)

Unfold a pastry sheet on a parchment-lined baking sheet. Use a rolling pin to roll the dough into an 11 × 13-inch rectangle, flattening slightly. With a small paring knife, score a ¼-inch border along the inside of the rectangle. Prick all over with a fork and then refrigerate for 30 minutes.

Preheat the oven to 400°F.

Cover the dough with a sheet of parchment paper and then add enough pie weights or dried beans to fill the crust. Bake until light golden brown, about 12 minutes. Use a fork to pierce any bubbles that may have formed and then let the pastry cool slightly on the baking sheet.

In a large bowl, whisk the eggs, half-and-half, thyme, salt and pepper, and half the scallions. Whisk in the cream cheese until smooth. Pour the egg mixture inside the border of the pastry. Top with the bacon, goat cheese, and asparagus.

Bake until the pastry is puffed and golden and the topping is set, 15 to 20 minutes. Cool for 5 minutes and then sprinkle with the remaining scallions and Maldon sea salt, if using. Cut into squares and serve.

SUNSHINE GRANOLA

Packed with orange-soaked fruits, toasted nuts, and coconut, this healthy granola tastes like sunshine to me—the ingredients combine to create a slightly tropical flavor. It's also a really fun recipe to make with kids, since it basically involves combining lots of yummy ingredients together and tossing them around before cooking. Your brunch guests will love waking up the day after the party and eating this for breakfast (or a midnight snack!).

MAKES 10 CUPS

5 tablespoons unsalted butter

⅓ cup (packed) light brown sugar

3 tablespoons honey

1 teaspoon ground cinnamon

1½ teaspoons pure vanilla extract

1 teaspoon kosher salt

4 cups old-fashioned (not quick-cooking) rolled oats

½ cup grated unsweetened coconut flakes

1 cup shelled raw pistachios

1 cup raw slivered almonds

½ sunflower seeds

¼ cup flaxseeds

Grated zest from 1 large orange

1 cup dried apple slices, chopped

1 cup dried apricots, chopped

½ cup golden raisins

1 cup fresh orange juice

Preheat the oven to 275°F. Line a large rimmed baking sheet with parchment paper and lightly spray with cooking spray.

In a small saucepan over low heat, bring the butter, sugar, honey, cinnamon, vanilla, and salt to a simmer. Stir until the sugar is dissolved and then set aside.

In a very large mixing bowl, combine the oats, coconut flakes, pistachios, almonds, sunflower seeds, flaxseeds, and grated orange zest. Pour the butter-sugar mixture over the top and use a large mixing spoon to toss it all around. You want to make sure that all the oats are lightly coated.

Spread the oat mixture onto the prepared baking sheet and bake for 1 hour and 10 minutes, stirring halfway through for even cooking.

Meanwhile, combine the apple slices, apricots, and raisins in a medium bowl. Pour the orange juice over the top, toss to combine, and let stand for 1 hour.

Remove the baking sheet from the oven, drain the fruit, and then add it to the granola. Stir well and then bake for an additional 10 minutes. Set aside to cool (the granola will get crispy when it's completely cooled). Store in an airtight container for up to 2 weeks or in the freezer for up to 1 month.

28

FIESTA DINNER PARTY

The first trip that Adam and I ever took together was to the Riviera Maya, outside Cancún. I'll never forget the feeling of being in the throes of an early romance (though we both knew this was something special) and arriving at our *casita* on a private beach after a very late flight. Thanks to a series of plane delays, the restaurant was closed by the time we arrived, but the hotel sent up a tray of the best tacos I'd ever eaten and a bottle of wine, and we ate them on our terrace against a background of night sky and crashing waves. I'm not sure if it was the stunning setting, the romantic company, or simply the fact that I was starving after a long day of travel, but I remember it as one of the best meals I've ever had.

We've since gone back to Mexico several times, and I only fall more and more in love with the vibrant decor, sculptural cacti, and most of all, the food. It's a good thing we live in Austin, where people think nothing of eating Mexican cuisine on a weekly (if

not daily) basis, and tortillas, avocados, and jalapeños are constant staples in my kitchen. Since there's just something about margaritas and guacamole that screams "party," during the spring and summer months our weekends are full of friends popping by for impromptu get-togethers with south-of-the-border flavor.

This year, I wanted to welcome the balmier temperatures by throwing a fiesta-themed dinner party. There's an amazing little Mexican import and garden shop inside one of my favorite plant nurseries in East Austin, and I thought it would make a surprising and fun location for a "pop up"–style gathering, especially since it meant adorning our table with succulents and cacti pulled straight from the nursery shelves. A long wooden table dressed with Mexican textiles and colorful mismatched dishes was the focal point of our dinner, and a self-serve margarita bar got the party started the minute guests arrived.

Camille

The
MENU
FIESTA DINNER PARTY

For this casual, laid-back dinner, I created a Latin-inflected menu meant for sharing, with everything served on big family-style platters spread across the table. There's something about letting guests help themselves to the food that creates a relaxed vibe—plus, they can fill their plates with exactly what they want and go back for seconds if they'd like!

Hanger or flank steak is a perfect choice for parties—it's practically foolproof on the grill and can be thinly sliced for layering in tacos or simply eaten as is. I dial the flavor way up on this one by serving it with an addictive chimichurri sauce—it's the South American answer to pesto, bursting with bright herbs and garlic. A refreshing salad with tons of crunch and my favorite sriracha-spiked, messy grilled street corn are the ideal accompaniments. An added bonus? It all tastes just as good at room temperature as it does straight off the grill, meaning I can hang out and drink margaritas with my guests before we all take our seats!

COCKTAILS AND APPETIZERS	FAMILY-STYLE FEAST	SOMETHING SWEET
TRADITIONAL LIME MARGARITAS, WATERMELON MARGARITAS, PAGE 267, MEXICAN BEER	SRIRACHA-SPIKED STREET CORN, PAGE 227	POPSICLES SOAKED IN CAVA
PERFECT GUACAMOLE, PAGE 226	HANGER STEAK WITH CHIMICHURRI AND GRILLED ONIONS, PAGE 228	WATERMELON WEDGES WITH SALT
	ARUGULA SALAD WITH JICAMA, HEIRLOOM TOMATOES, AVOCADO, AND QUESO FRESCO, PAGE 231	

For this gathering, I was inspired by a summer sunset and used mainly red, coral, and a few pops of yellow.

GET THE LOOK

This design is all about the mix of high and low, old and new, colorful and neutral. I started with the vibrant shades and bold patterns of Mexico by dressing the table in a vivid textile. Remember that tables don't have to be topped by actual tablecloths—I used an exotic bedsheet borrowed from my friend Jordan, and I've also used curtains, blankets, and upholstery as unexpected table coverings.

Next, I balanced out the busyness with simple white dinnerware and an all-green succulent centerpiece for a cool Austin-style vibe. Steak knives in a rainbow of hues really popped when paired with vintage silverware, and striped linen napkins added another layer of texture and perfectly mismatched pattern.

When working with a very colorful palette, I tend to choose either a warmer collection of reds, pinks, corals, and yellows *or* a cooler pattern of blues, greens, and purples. Sticking with either one or the other brings a cohesiveness to the design so that it doesn't feel random . . . or as though a rainbow exploded on the table. For this gathering, I was inspired by a summer sunset and used mainly red, coral, and a few pops of yellow.

Even for the most casual gatherings, a printed element on the table shows that a little extra effort went into making it feel like an occasion. Place cards are great because they allow the host to plan the perfect seating arrangement in advance, and menu cards are a nice way to give your guests an idea of what they'll be enjoying during the meal. I usually choose one or the other, since having both at each place setting can be overkill. My friend Emma of Antiquaria Design Studio designed these fantastic menu cards dotted with cacti, and you could easily design and print your own version by feeding heavy card stock through a home printer and cutting it to size.

bottoms up!

I set up a self-serve bar that doubled as a beautiful focal point with its colorful selection of Mexican drinks. When serving cocktails at a party, I'm a huge fan of mixing up an entire pitcher or punch bowl in advance (and stashing a backup in the fridge) so that I'm not left making everyone's drinks the entire night . . . I'd rather be drinking *with* them! I kept things classic by making my tried-and-true traditional lime margaritas and then mixed it up with a refreshing watermelon version, too.

HOMEGROWN CENTERPIECE

Since our pop-up party happened in a plant nursery, it was only fitting that we scooped up planted cacti and succulents from the nursery shelves to adorn our table.

Here are a few tips for working with succulents.

1 | *Before creating an arrangement, submerge the plants in a large bucket of soapy water to get rid of any dirt or bugs that might be lingering on the leaves.*

2 | *Fill the low vessel with a layer of gravel to encourage drainage and then add a layer of cactus potting soil deep enough to cover the succulents' roots.*

3 | *Arrange your succulents in the soil, making sure the roots are tucked in. Then pour sand or river rocks on top of the soil for a finished look.*

4 | *Water immediately, then place in a sunny spot and water every couple of weeks. The good thing is, if you tend to forget to water your plants as I do, succulents are the way to go. These guys can survive almost anything!*

SECRETS TO THE PERFECT MARGARITAS

I've sampled margaritas at just about every Mexican spot in town (it's a tough job, but someone's gotta do it!), and when I taste a really great one, I do my best to convince the bartender to spill his secrets. A few things I've learned for mixing the perfect margarita:

1 | *Keep it pure. Ditch the syrupy-sweet triple sec or sweet-and-sour mix in favor of light agave nectar. The amount of sweetness can be adjusted to your liking, and agave's clean flavor lets freshly squeezed lime juice take center stage.*

2 | *Keep it simple. My classic margarita recipe has only three ingredients—tequila, lime juice, agave nectar—and my Watermelon Margaritas (pictured on page 256) need only the addition of fruit.*

3 | *Half salty, half not. Instead of coating the entire rims of glasses with salt, try salting only half; it's a great way to get the salty, addictive flavor without totally overpowering the drink. Simply moisten half of the outer rim of a glass with a lime wedge and dip the glass, upside down at an angle, into a saucer full of kosher salt.*

THE FAVORS

I spotted these mini-bottles of tequila at a liquor store a while back and immediately stocked up on a few so I could hand them out at my next Tex-Mex get-together. I don't know a single person who doesn't love a good margarita, so what could be better than sending guests home with the makings for their own? I paired the bottles with a cute little key lime and popped it all in a drawstring bag imprinted with the word *¡Olé!* Here's what you need to make your own:

Small muslin drawstring bags (available at craft stores)

A rubber stamp with a fun Spanish word or phrase (there are great sources online for practically any rubber stamps you can dream up!)

An ink pad in a color that coordinates with your fiesta palette

Mini-bottles of tequila and key limes

Simply stamp each bag, allow to dry, and fill with tequila-shot fixin's!

THE BEATS

My friend Jenn brought her cool vintage turntable, and guests played DJ and sorted through her assortment of new and old Latin-inflected albums. Whether you're using a turntable or an iPod, these are some of my favorite artists to crank up at a fiesta.

Rodrigo y Gabriela

Gipsy Kings

Sidestepper (especially their song "Paloma")

Elastic Bond (check out "Pierdo el Control," "In Your Eyes," and "Son Pa' Ti")

Gotan Project

Cilantro Boombox (love the track "La Batalla")

Grupo Fantasma

Bebel Gilberto

Ray Barretto ("El Watusi" is a great pick)

La Santa Cecilia

Juanes

PERFECT GUACAMOLE

As a guacamole fanatic, I've experimented with making it just about every way imaginable: with and without tomatoes, chunky and smooth, even topped with exotic ingredients like pomegranate seeds and crabmeat. One day I decided to take everything I'd learned from my years of guacamole making and hone it all down to the perfect, classic recipe. And it turned out to be the one that makes everyone beg for more.

MAKES 1 ½ CUPS

¼ cup chopped white onion

1 jalapeño, chopped (include the seeds if you like extra heat)

2 tablespoons chopped fresh cilantro

1 garlic clove, minced

1 large avocado, halved and pitted

2 teaspoons freshly squeezed lime juice

¾ teaspoon kosher salt

¼ cup diced tomato

1 tablespoon cotija cheese

Using a mortar and pestle, combine the onion, jalapeño, cilantro, and garlic. Using a paring knife, cut a crisscross pattern into the meat of the avocado and then use a big spoon to scoop the cubes into the mortar and pestle. Add the lime juice and salt and mash everything together. I like to leave a rough consistency, but if you prefer a smoother texture, puree in a blender.

Gently fold the tomatoes into the guacamole. Sprinkle with cotija and serve.

BITS OF BRILLIANCE:
Why not set up a make-your-own corn station at your next backyard barbecue? Some of my other favorite toppings for grilled corn include the following:

Roasted garlic mixed with butter + Chopped fresh herbs such as chives, parsley, and oregano

Truffle oil + Grated Parmesan + A squeeze of lemon juice

Sun-dried tomatoes blended with softened butter + Thinly sliced basil

SRIRACHA-SPIKED STREET CORN

Once fresh corn hits supermarket shelves, this is the way I can't stop making (and eating) it: for lunches, dinners, happy hours, barbecues, with friends . . . I've never met a guest who didn't ask for the recipe! So here it is, in all its ridiculously simple glory. Don't be alarmed by the fact that a fair amount of mayonnaise is involved, and do not, I repeat do not, substitute yogurt as some healthy-minded cooks (me) might be tempted to do. And did I mention that it's highly addictive? Consider this your fair warning . . .

MAKES 8 HALF-EAR PORTIONS

Extra-virgin olive oil

4 ears fresh corn, shucked and cut in half

Garlic salt

⅓ cup mayonnaise (I like classic Hellmann's)

1 tablespoon sriracha sauce

Fresh-squeezed lime juice

1 bunch fresh cilantro, roughly chopped

2 tablespoons chili powder

Maldon sea salt

3 limes, each cut into 6 wedges

Pour a bit of oil on a small plate and roll the corn in it to coat evenly. Sprinkle all over with garlic salt.

Heat a grill or grill pan to high and grill the corn until slightly charred, about 5 minutes. Turn occasionally to cook on all sides.

In a small bowl, combine the mayonnaise, sriracha, and a squeeze of lime juice. Whisk to combine.

When the corn comes off the grill, slather it with the mayonnaise mixture, then sprinkle with cilantro, chili powder, and the Maldon sea salt. Roll the corn around in the mixture to get it all evenly coated, and serve with slices of lime so guests can squeeze more juice as they like.

Embrace the messiness . . . I promise, it's worth it.

HANGER STEAK WITH CHIMICHURRI AND GRILLED ONIONS

Hanger and flank steaks are an entertainer's secret weapons: extremely affordable cuts of meat that when soaked in this sweet and spicy marinade take on a flavor that rivals any tenderloin or filet. I love to make tacos out of the steak, onions, and chimichurri; my gluten-free guests enjoy theirs sans tortilla.

SERVES 8

MARINADE

5 garlic cloves, minced

6 green onions, sliced

⅓ cup soy sauce

2 tablespoons agave nectar

2 tablespoons sesame oil (or extra-virgin olive oil in a pinch)

Zest and juice of 1 lime

1 tablespoon crushed red pepper flakes

½ teaspoon cayenne (optional; use if you desire extra heat)

STEAK

2 pounds hanger or flank steak, trimmed

Canola oil

Kosher salt and freshly ground black pepper

3 red onions, cut into ¾-inch-thick rounds

1 large bunch fresh cilantro

CHIMICHURRI

½ cup red wine vinegar

½ cup sherry vinegar

⅓ cup extra-virgin olive oil

1 teaspoon light agave nectar

1 shallot, minced

2 garlic cloves, minced

¼ cup chopped fresh flat-leaf parsley

⅓ cup chopped fresh cilantro

2 tablespoons chopped fresh chives

Squeeze of lime juice

Kosher salt and freshly ground black pepper

Corn tortillas, 6-inch

To make the marinade, combine all the ingredients in a small bowl. Transfer to a large resealable plastic bag, add the steak, and turn to coat. Refrigerate for at least 2 hours or overnight.

To make the chimichurri, in a small bowl, whisk together the vinegars, oil, and agave nectar. Add the remaining ingredients, whisk to combine, and let stand at room temperature for about 1 hour (or refrigerate overnight and bring to room temperature before serving).

Remove the steak from the marinade and discard the marinade. Pat to dry and then brush with a bit of canola oil and season generously on both sides with kosher salt and freshly ground black pepper. Press the seasonings into the steak to adhere.

In a medium bowl, toss the onion rings with a bit of canola oil just to coat and season well with salt and pepper.

Preheat the grill to medium-high. Grill the steak about 6 minutes per side for medium-rare. Remove from the heat and let rest, loosely covered, for 5 minutes to let the juices redistribute.

Meanwhile, add the onion rings to the grill and grill for 5 minutes, turning occasionally, until tender and slightly charred. During the last 2 minutes of cooking, toss the tortillas on the grill and cook for 1 minute on each side.

Slice meat across the grain and serve it on a large platter with the cilantro, grilled red onions, and chimichurri.

SOURCES

Location: Hijo at Jardineros Nursery
Floral design: The Nouveau Romantics
Food styling: Meghan Erwin
Paper goods: Antiquaria
Table & benches: Liv by Design
Wardrobe: JM Drygoods
Tabletop pieces & linens: Anthropologie

ARUGULA SALAD WITH JICAMA, HEIRLOOM TOMATOES, AVOCADO, AND QUESO FRESCO

This salad is my own little celebration of springtime produce: the more vibrant colors that get tossed in, the better! It has an undeniably fresh quality, since all the ingredients are raw, but the crunchy jicama and radishes are the perfect foil for creamy arugula and queso fresco, making this salad a real party in your mouth. Look for heirloom tomatoes in the oddest colors and gnarliest shapes you can find; they add so much character!

SERVES 8

AGAVE LIME VINAIGRETTE

Zest and juice of 2 limes (¼ cup)

Zest and juice of ½ orange (¼ cup)

1 shallot, minced

1½ tablespoons light agave nectar

⅓ cup extra-virgin olive oil

Kosher salt and freshly ground black pepper

SALAD

4 heirloom tomatoes of assorted colors, sliced into thick wedges

1 cup thin 1-inch-long jicama sticks

6 radishes, cleaned, stems removed, and thinly shaved on a mandoline

3 ears fresh corn, shucked

Kosher salt and freshly ground black pepper

2 large avocados, halved, pitted, and sliced

8 cups baby arugula

½ cup crumbled queso fresco

¼ cup roasted pumpkin seeds (see "How to Toast Nuts" on page 47)

To make the dressing, in a small bowl, combine the lime zest and juice, orange zest and juice, and shallot. Let sit for 10 minutes. Whisk in the agave nectar and then slowly whisk in the oil. Season with salt and pepper and set aside.

In a large bowl, combine the tomatoes, jicama, and radishes. With a sharp knife, remove the corn kernels from the cobs and add them to the bowl. Add half of the vinaigrette, season with salt and pepper, and toss to combine.

Add the avocados and arugula and gently toss, taking care not to smash the avocados. Top with crumbled queso fresco, pumpkin seeds, a drizzle of vinaigrette, and a bit more salt and pepper, and serve.

summer

HAPPY CAMPERS A HUSBAND AND WIFE WITH A LOVE

>>>>>>>>> EMBRACING THE SEASON <<<<<<<<<

SIGHTS, SOUNDS, AND TASTES OF SUMMER

I would definitely call myself a summer girl—it's the season I most look forward to all year long. When I was growing up, my end-of-May birthday usually fell during the last week of school, and even now the day represents *freedom* in my mind: the time to lighten up and have some fun! There's nothing like that first dip in the pool that recalls sunny childhood memories and gets me in the mood to ditch work early for a picnic in the park complete with cold fried chicken, juicy strawberries, and fresh-squeezed lemonade. This is the season for unfussy, effortless entertaining; fine china and perfectly arranged flowers just don't feel right!

Since it's way too hot here in Texas to spend hours sweating in the kitchen, my summertime menus usually revolve around dishes with simple, bold flavors that can be tossed on the grill and require almost no cleanup. Plus, open-fire cooking usually gets Adam in on the action, which means that I have time to kick back with a margarita and catch up with guests while he cooks.

At its heart, summertime is really all about feeling carefree, and I do my best to carve out entire days when I turn off my laptop and focus on family and friends. Easier said than done if you're a fellow Type A personality, but I encourage you to embrace this season when the kids are out of school, demanding clients go on vacation, and there's a slower pace at the office. You deserve a break, too, and just think how much more productive you'll be if you allow yourself to recharge and have some fun! Are you with me? Here's how I get in a summery state of mind.

Camille

HERE'S HOW I CONNECT WITH ALL THE SENSES TO USHER IN THE SUMMER SEASON:

TEXTURE.

If there's ever a time to don a casual hostess outfit, summer is it. A linen caftan with exotic detailing is incredibly chic when paired with bare feet. Even when an occasion calls for something a bit more pulled together, my propensity to pair flat metallic sandals with a simple printed shift dress means all-night comfort and is particularly useful if I end up walking on sand or grass as summer often requires. Think in terms of light, breathable fabrics like cotton and linen when dressing yourself, as well as your table, for a dinner party. I have a collection of light blankets from India and Mexico that I repurpose as the most gorgeous tablecloths—their vibrant colors and textures feel festive without trying too hard and are bold enough to set the tone for an entire celebration. At home, I've always been obsessed with textures and shapes that recall marine life: the wild shapes of sea coral, spiral patterns of shells, and roughness of sand are all so beautiful, and I place elements I've scavenged from past beach vacations around the house to instantly take me away.

SCENT.

My signature perfume throughout the year is called "At the Beach 1966," and it smells like Coppertone, salt water, and ocean air. Every time I catch a whiff, I'm instantly transported to a golden summer day where I'm playing in the sand and surf without a care in the world! Try hanging your sheets outside to dry for an authentic "fresh linen" fragrance that can never be replicated with dryer sheets. Make a nontoxic window cleaner by combining equal parts white vinegar and water, plus the fresh juice of 2 lemons, and spread a natural citrus scent as you clean. Grow pots of herbs in a sunny kitchen window for an edible indoor garden that perfumes the entire room with delicious, summery aromas.

COLOR.

I love the look of all white against sun-kissed skin when I'm getting dressed in the summertime . . . but when dressing my *table* for a party, summer is when I really embrace color. Rather than sticking to a limited palette, I usually choose either all cool shades (blues, greens, lavender) or all warm shades (pinks, reds, oranges)—and then go to town! Layer different patterns such as florals and stripes in striking color combinations for a bold look and then pile on vibrant dishes, mismatched napkins, and colorful cocktails. I love pieces that incorporate textural or exotic touches like woven Guatemalan patterns or Indian-inspired tassels to satisfy the wanderlust that strikes more frequently in the summertime. If the minimalist in you is cringing at the thought of all that color, try sticking with a neutral palette and adding one vibrant pop. My bright teal tablecloth always makes a statement in our dining room that's otherwise cream, white, and light wood.

TASTE.

Summer is a constant reminder of the earth's generosity: just take a stroll past farmers' market stalls brimming with juicy peaches, heirloom tomatoes in every shade, summer squash begging to be tossed on the grill, and the thing I look forward to all year long: sweet slices of watermelon just waiting to be sprinkled with sea salt and devoured. I make tons of salads during the summer and usually take my inspiration from my market haul to dream up new flavor marriages that combine both raw and cooked ingredients. Many of them can be served at room temperature, allowing me to set out a big platter and let guests help themselves at a leisurely pace.

30

SETTING THE SUMMER TABLE

As the long days of summer approach, I inevitably catch a serious case of wanderlust that refuses to be ignored. And since booking a flight to the nearest tropical paradise isn't always in the cards, I find myself bringing the vibrant colors and spicy style of exotic locales into my home to satisfy my longings for adventure. One of the many reasons I love designing tabletops is that they allow me a quick and noncommittal way to shake up a room and explore the boundaries of decor beyond my usual style. Summer is the perfect time to go bold with color and pattern, and since alfresco dining can get awfully hot here in Austin, I love starting the day with a beautifully set breakfast table that lets us enjoy the sunshine before temps hit the triple digits. I designed this look with out-of-town guests in mind: as everyone wakes up, they'll lazily gather one by one around a colorful table set in shades of a summer sunrise. Fresh berries, a basket of croissants, and hot coffee await, and the only dress code requirement is bare feet.

Camille

PALETTE.

Coral, watermelon, apricot, tomato.

LINENS.

Bold coral stripes in linen and cotton grace a floor-length tablecloth that becomes a vibrant foundation for the rest of the table. A paisley runner, hand-blocked in India, adds a cheerful, not-too-matchy layer, and gauzy white linen napkins bring a touch of neutral relief.

CENTERPIECE.

A footed compote in white ceramic is a classic piece to add to your collection: it elevates any floral arrangement and allows the flowers to gracefully drape over the edge of the vessel. After adding a ball of chicken wire for stability, we filled it with ruffly celosia and thistle, pink ranunculus, and the most romantic peach-colored stock. Next came that jaw-dropping 'Coral Charm' peony—truly the star of the show! Jasmine vine, peony leaves, and silverberry foliage add fullness. The overall look recalls the bright shades of summer produce—juicy berries, peppery radishes, and cherry groves.

PLACE SETTINGS.

The bright yellow rim on these glazed ceramics is happiness on a plate, providing the perfect, sunny way to welcome the day! I paired them with coral porcelain bowls for an unexpected warm-hued complement; filling them with berries makes each setting look so inviting. It doesn't get more classic than Picardie glasses (the standard in Parisian cafes), which lend a casual, easygoing vibe when filled with fresh juice.

THE DETAILS.

For an unexpected splash of color, I picked up a bunch of vibrant pink radishes at the farmers' market, then used twine to tie one onto each napkin. It's an easy little touch that adds major impact, and I love how it imbues the entire look with an organic, farm-to-table quality.

SOURCES

Location: CTC Garden
Floral design: The Nouveau Romantics
Calligraphy: Kathryn Murray Calligraphy
Furniture: Loot Vintage Rentals
Tabletop pieces: Anthropologie

CHAPTER

31

SUMMER SALADS

I have a sneaking suspicion that most people generally think of salads as major bummers. Maybe they still associate them with tasteless iceberg, out-of-season tomatoes, and so-called bacon bits, but I am here to say that when done right, salads can be inspiring, bursting with flavor, and downright obsession worthy. And they don't even need to include lettuce! To me, the idea of salad has come to represent a way of life that revolves around eating seasonally and deliciously, which is why I have some version of a salad nearly every day for lunch. When I'm at the farmers' market on the weekends, I don't have to worry about knowing "what in the world I'm going to cook with this [insert unusual produce here]," since I know that I can toss it into a midweek salad and experience a new flavor adventure. The key to making and enjoying great salads is using the highest-quality in-season ingredients you can get your hands on and then combining those items to create a mix of sweet-tart-salty, crunchy-creamy—in other words, balanced flavors, interesting textures, and brilliant color. After a week of indulgence, there's nothing that tastes better than a farm-fresh salad of crunchy, raw vegetables . . . but it's amazing what a few slices of creamy avocado and a handful of sweet currants and toasted walnuts do to elevate the experience. And while I eat my fair share of salads all year round, they really shine when summer produce reaches its peak and I can choose from the bounty of sweet melons, heirloom tomatoes, and an abundance of herbs at the market—often, a squeeze of lemon, a drizzle of extra-virgin olive oil, salt, and freshly ground black pepper are all that's needed to enhance their perfect flavors.

In this chapter, I'm sharing four of my all-time favorite summer salads that are simple enough to toss together for a quick weeknight meal and interesting enough to add to the spread when friends come for Sunday lunch (they'll be begging for the recipes). One of my favorite things about salads is that you can use the recipes as general guidelines to get inspired and then change them up depending on what's in your fridge and your own flashes of culinary genius. I hope that you'll use my four salad "MVPs" as jumping-off points for your own creations. And when you keep an eye on balancing flavor, texture, and color, you're sure to end up with something delicious. While each of these recipes combines drastically different elements, all of them turn "eating your veggies" into a real summertime treat.

Camille

AUSTIN SALAD

This combination of raw and cooked ingredients was inspired by Austin's health-loving, "keeping it weird" culture that's been around since my parents went to college here in the seventies. It's a vegetarian salad that's substantial enough for a meal: crunchy raw vegetables combined with creamy avocado, nutty farro, and garbanzo beans provide loads of protein and many essential nutrients, and the currants add an unexpected hint of sweetness.

SERVES 4

MARINATED SHALLOT VINAIGRETTE

2 tablespoons diced shallots

2 tablespoons good-quality Dijon mustard

2 teaspoons honey

¼ cup sherry vinegar

½ cup extra-virgin olive oil

Kosher salt and freshly ground black pepper

SALAD

½ cup currants

1 cup cooked farro, cooled (feel free to substitute other whole grains, such as quinoa or barley)

1 cup sunflower sprouts

½ cup Marcona almonds, chopped

1 cup radishes, cleaned, stems removed, and sliced very thinly or shaved on a mandoline

1 head butter lettuce, torn into bite-size pieces

1 cup canned garbanzo beans, rinsed very well and drained

2 ripe but firm avocados

6 to 8 chives

Coarse sea salt

To make the vinaigrette, in a small bowl, whisk together the shallots, Dijon, honey, and vinegar. Slowly stream in the oil while whisking and then season to taste with salt and pepper. Let marinate for at least 30 minutes to allow the shallot to soften. Keep sealed in an airtight jar in the refrigerator for up to 1 week.

In a small bowl, cover the currants with warm water. Set aside to let them plump while you make the rest of the salad.

In a large bowl, combine the farro, sprouts, almonds, radishes, lettuce, and garbanzo beans. Add just enough dressing to lightly coat everything and toss to combine. Peel and slice the avocados and add them to the bowl. Use cooking shears to snip 1-inch sections of the chives over the top.

Drain the currants and sprinkle them evenly over the salad. Toss lightly and then drizzle with a little more dressing and a big pinch of sea salt.

BEETS AND GRAPEFRUIT

A few years ago on a trip to LA, Adam and I had one of the most perfect dinners at Wolfgang Puck's iconic Beverly Hills steakhouse, CUT. The Wagyu beef was transcendent, but I was surprised to discover that my favorite part of the meal was actually the salad—a roasted beet, grapefruit, and avocado creation, artfully composed and topped with pistachios and microgreens. I took a few liberties with Chef Puck's masterpiece by using a mixture of red and golden beets, tangy French feta, and sweet tangerines to counter the grapefruit's bitterness. Choose uniform-size beets so that they cook evenly.

SERVES 4

SALAD

4 medium red beets, scrubbed and trimmed

4 medium golden beets, scrubbed and trimmed

1 large grapefruit

2 tangerines

1 bunch fresh mint

4 ounces French feta (not crumbled)

¼ cup shelled pistachios, roughly chopped

½ cup microgreens

Coarse sea salt and freshly ground black pepper

HONEY-BALSAMIC VINAIGRETTE

2 tablespoons balsamic vinegar

2 teaspoons honey

¼ cup extra-virgin olive oil

Kosher salt and freshly ground black pepper

Preheat the oven to 425°F. Wrap the beets in a large foil packet, and tightly crimp the edges to seal. Place on a baking sheet and roast for 1 hour, or until the beets are tender (to check, slide a knife into the side of the largest beet—when it slides in with no resistance, the beets are ready). Set the beets aside to cool and then use a paper towel to rub the skin off each beet. Cut the beets into wedges.

Cut the top and bottom off each end of the grapefruit so it can stand upright on your cutting board. Use a sharp paring knife to cut the peel off the sides, following the natural curves of the fruit, making sure to remove as much white pith as possible. Segment the grapefruit by carefully cutting along the membranes that divide each one, separating each grapefruit segment as you go.

Remove the peel from the tangerines and then use a serrated knife to slice each one into thin rounds.

Remove the mint leaves from the stems, discarding the stems.

On each of four salad plates, arrange an even amount of beet wedges, grapefruit segments, tangerine rounds, and mint leaves. Thinly slice the feta and tuck a few slices into the ingredients on each plate. Sprinkle the pistachios and microgreens over the top.

To make the vinaigrette, whisk together the balsamic vinegar and honey and then slowly whisk in the oil. Season to taste with salt and pepper and drizzle the dressing over each salad, using as much or as little as you prefer. Store extra dressing in an airtight container in the refrigerator for up to 1 week.

Check the seasoning and add a little sea salt and freshly ground black pepper to the top of each salad.

SEARED TUNA NIÇOISE

Ah, Salade Niçoise . . . Anytime I encounter one on a restaurant menu, my decision's been made. The classic combination of tomatoes, haricots verts, potatoes, briny olives, and perfectly hard-cooked eggs creates one of my favorite salads of all time, and this one swaps out the typical canned tuna for herb-crusted seared ahi, which takes it to a new level.

SERVES 4

SALAD

½ pound small potatoes, scrubbed

2 tablespoons extra-virgin olive oil

Kosher salt and freshly ground black pepper

1 teaspoon herbes de Provence (see page 111)

1 pound fresh sushi-quality tuna (thawed if frozen and kept very cold in the refrigerator)

½ pound haricots verts or thin green beans, trimmed

1 pint cherry tomatoes, halved or quartered if large

2 romaine hearts, leaves separated, washed, and dried

1 cup pitted mixed oil-marinated olives, drained

4 hard-boiled eggs, peeled and sliced

DIJON VINAIGRETTE

3 tablespoons lemon juice

2 tablespoons Dijon mustard

1 garlic clove, minced

⅓ cup extra-virgin olive oil

Kosher salt and freshly ground black pepper

Preheat the oven to 400°F and line a baking sheet with foil.

In a medium bowl, toss the potatoes with 1 tablespoon of the oil, salt and pepper, and herbes de Provence. Spread out on the prepared baking sheet and roast until tender when pierced with a fork, about 25 minutes. Remove from the oven and let cool.

Meanwhile, liberally season the tuna on all sides with salt and pepper and herbes de Provence. Heat the remaining 1 tablespoon of oil in a cast-iron skillet over high heat.

Carefully place the tuna in the skillet and allow to sear for 30 seconds. Using tongs, turn the tuna to sear the sides and ends for 30 seconds each. Set aside on a plate to cool while you make the rest of the salad.

To make the vinaigrette, in a small bowl, whisk together the lemon juice, Dijon, and garlic. Slowly whisk in the oil and then season to taste with salt and pepper.

Bring a medium pot of salted water to a boil. Add the haricots verts and blanch until tender but crisp, about 4 minutes. Drain in a colander and run under cold water to stop the cooking. Transfer to a clean bowl and season with 1 tablespoon of the vinaigrette and salt and pepper to taste.

In another bowl, season the tomatoes with 1 tablespoon of the vinaigrette and salt and pepper to taste.

In a large salad bowl, season the romaine leaves with 1 tablespoon vinaigrette and salt and pepper to taste.

On a large platter, arrange the romaine leaves, haricots verts, tomatoes, potatoes, olives, and eggs. Cut the tuna into ¾-inch slices and add to the platter. Drizzle the remaining dressing over the salad and let everyone help themselves.

SUMMER MARKET SALAD

When my farmers' market bag is brimming with a bumper crop of late-summer corn, zucchini, and basil, I make this salad. The crunchy, sweet sugar snaps are a refreshing contrast to charred zucchini, and a big wedge of Parmesan shaved over the top just before serving provides a salty finish. Serve with an ice-cold bottle of crisp rosé.

SERVES 4

SALAD

2 small or 1 large zucchini, cut on the diagonal into ½-inch slices

Extra-virgin olive oil

1 cup sugar snap peas, ends trimmed and strings removed if needed

6 handfuls baby arugula

¼ cup basil leaves, torn

1 ear fresh corn, shucked

Wedge of Parmesan

Coarse sea salt and freshly ground black pepper

CITRUS VINAIGRETTE

Zest and juice of 1 orange (¼ cup)

Zest and juice of 1 lemon (¼ cup)

1 tablespoon Dijon mustard

¼ cup extra-virgin olive oil

Kosher salt and freshly ground black pepper

Heat a grill or a grill pan to medium-high heat. Lightly brush both sides of the zucchini slices with olive oil. Grill until lightly charred on both sides but still crisp, about 2 minutes per side. Remove to a large bowl and let cool.

Meanwhile, make the vinaigrette by whisking together the orange zest and juice, lemon zest and juice, and Dijon mustard. Slowly whisk in the oil and then season to taste with salt and pepper.

When the zucchini is cooled to room temperature, add the sugar snap peas, arugula, and basil to the bowl. Stand the ear of corn upright on a cutting board and use a sharp knife to cut the kernels from the cob. Add the corn to the salad.

Toss with enough dressing to lightly coat the arugula and then use a vegetable peeler to shave large shards of Parmesan over the top. Season the salad with sea salt and pepper and serve.

32

TAKING IT OUTDOORS

You can bet that, as a former event planner, I've witnessed my fair share of outdoor parties that would make even the most intrepid hostess think twice about hosting a gathering outside. For starters, there was that swanky fete in downtown Austin where all the VIP cabanas lifted off the ground and *literally* blew away when the wind picked up. Then there was the formal wedding for three hundred guests, where a torrential downpour left every last one of them soaked to the bone. And I'll never forget the cocktail party on the hotel rooftop, where a blustering wind blew through and left the DJ's equipment lying in a heap in the middle of the dance floor.

As memorable as these experiences were—they certainly made for some good stories!—I'm here to tell you that my very favorite way to entertain is *still* outside in the backyard (and, no, I'm not a glutton for punishment). When Adam and I built our house three years ago, we worked to create a space where our indoor lives

flowed seamlessly into the outdoors so we could spend as much time possible soaking up the sunshine and surrounding ourselves with nature. On most evenings from March to October, you can find us hanging out by the grill, enjoying a glass of wine while dinner practically prepares itself. When friends join us, I'll set the table simply with butcher paper (which can be thrown away postdinner), my softest linen napkins, stoneware plates, and a couple pots of herbs in the center. And nothing sets a more magical scene than lots of candles to light up the night when the sun goes down!

There's no denying that outdoor entertaining brings its own set of complications, but that's certainly no reason to miss out on the fun. With a little advance preparation and a few expert lessons I've picked up over the years (I learned them the hard way so that you don't have to!), you'll be spending your summer outdoors in the sunshine, surrounded by good friends and sated with great food . . . exactly as it *should* be.

Camille

1. KEEP YOUR GUESTS HYDRATED.

In the heat of the summer, guests will drink more cold beverages than you ever thought possible. Set up a drinks' station in a shaded area of the yard where guests can pour their own beverages and go back for refills as many times as they like. Mix and match glassware for a laid-back vibe, and include a couple of seasonal garnishes such as fresh herbs and berries to dress up cocktails. I love to fill large drink dispensers with lemonade and infuse water with cooling mint leaves and cucumber slices. They make the bar look amazing while ensuring that there's always a nonalcoholic option to quench guests' thirst.

2. THINK BEYOND THE COOLER.

Get creative with vessels when icing down bottled or canned drinks. Galvanized buckets, wine barrels, wagons, and wheelbarrows filled with ice will keep refreshments cool and collected all day while adding a summery visual element to any get-together.

3. PROTECT GUESTS FROM THE ELEMENTS.

Nothing's more of a buzz kill than mosquitos at a party. Keep bites at bay by setting up a station with galvanized metal beach buckets full of ice and stocked with insect repellent and bottles of sunscreen. For extra protection, spray the air, ground, and plants with an insect-repelling fogger several hours before the party.

4. CONSIDER FOOD TEMPS.

When I worked in catering, I quickly learned that when it comes to serving food outside on hot days, room temperature is best. Fresh crunchy salads, sliced grilled meats, and light sandwiches can hang out on a buffet for an hour without wilting in the heat. And most important, you won't be fighting the losing battle of trying to keep cold foods cold in the summer heat.

5. GET YOUR GAME ON.

Although summertime parties often call for nothing more than blue skies and a cool body of water, why not make things really lively by sparking a little friendly competition? Classic yard games like cornhole, washers, or bocce ball turn any backyard space into a playing field and keep guests of all ages entertained for hours. And who said that piñatas should be reserved for fiestas? I've had them made in shapes to fit just about every theme under the sun, from a watermelon wedge for a kid's birthday to a giant stiletto for a ladies'-night party. They're always a major hit, pun intended. If spontaneity is more your style, scatter a few hula hoops and beach balls in the yard and then sit back and watch the pickup games ensue.

6. KEEP IT SIMPLE.

Alfresco dinner parties call for no-fuss tabletops, but that doesn't mean you have to break out the disposable cups and throwaway plates! I like to keep it pretty and pared down with a natural linen runner, earthenware plates, and sturdy glassware. Let the table decor blend with the natural setting so that the great outdoors can take center stage.

7. DRESS IT UP.

For outdoor gatherings, I stick with a laid-back centerpiece that won't wilt in the heat. A big wooden bowl looks so cheerful when filled with lemons and limes, wildflowers gathered in mason jars make for a casual arrangement, and pots of herbs or succulents can be sent home with guests for impromptu party favors! And don't forget: when serving food family-style, beautiful platters filled with abundant food can be an inviting centerpiece all on their own.

8. FIRE IT UP.

My secret weapon that keeps postparty cleanup to a minimum? Cook as much on the grill as possible! Not only is grilled food delicious and oozing with summertime flavor, it cuts down on the number of pans and serving pieces that have to be washed at the end of the night. And since Adam loves to man the grill, it's a great activity for the guys to bond over, cold beers in hand.

9. CREATE AMBIENCE.

As the sun sets, create a magical glow with some strategically placed candles and lights. For Adam's birthday party a couple years ago, we surrounded the pool with tons of votive candles that lit up the night. String up white cafe lights overhead, place a few lanterns with candles inside around the patio, or scatter bamboo torches filled with citronella oil along the perimeter of the yard. They'll do double duty by warding off bugs while adding light!

10. END SWEETLY.

Pay homage to summer camping trips by inviting guests to gather around a bonfire to roast marshmallows and make s'mores (don't forget the guitars for impromptu sing-alongs!). Or capture the nostalgia of old-fashioned ice-cream parlors by setting up a make-your-own sundae bar where everyone can craft their dream creations. Fill large bowls with ice, nestle in two or three ice-cream flavors, and set out an endless array of toppings for an undeniable crowd-pleaser.

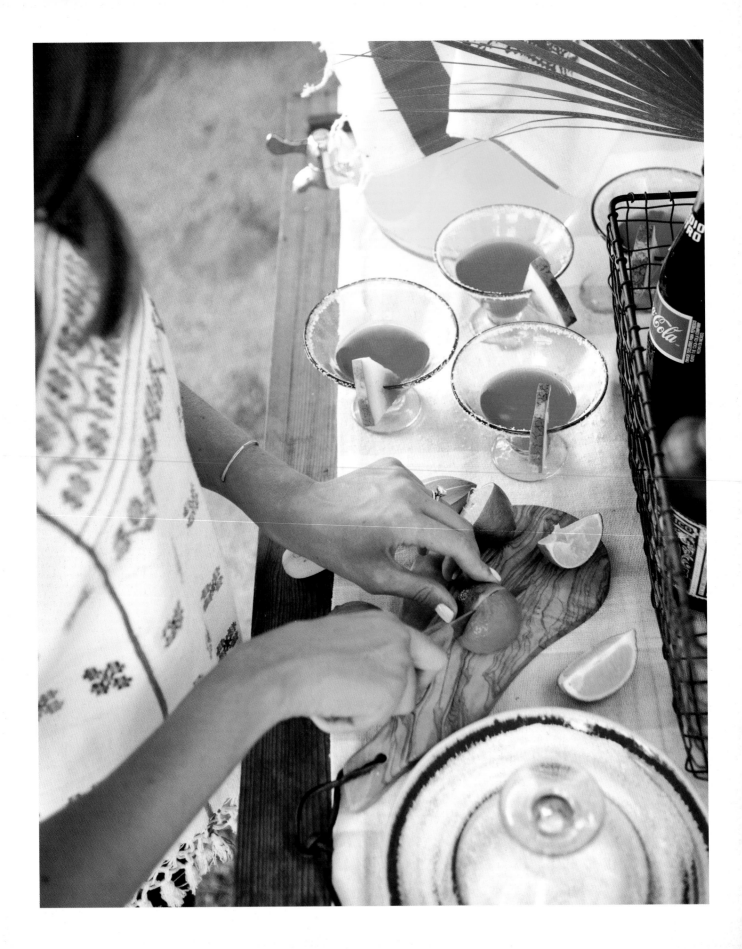

33

THE WELL-STOCKED HOME BAR

>>>>>>>>>> CARE FOR A DRINK? <<<<<<<<<<

It's one of the first sentences uttered when guests arrive, and having that drink in hand—even if it's just Pellegrino—instantly puts them at ease. Over time, I've built up a pretty well-stocked beverage area so that I'm prepared for just about any request my guests might have . . . and you might be surprised at just how easy it is to do! You don't have to be a wine connoisseur and you certainly don't have to be an expert mixologist to offer your guests delicious beverage options. All you need to do is have the right handful of items on hand, with a couple of signature cocktails up your sleeve when you want to pull out all the stops. The best part of having a well-stocked bar? You'll be set and ready for an impromptu celebration without having to rush out to the liquor store. Just open up your cabinet and break out the bubbly!

Here's what you need to have a "full bar" setup—and win the Best Hostess Ever Award in the process!

Camille

THE TOOLS

The first step to stocking the bar is making sure you've equipped your guests with everything they'll need to mix up their drink of choice. The following are the tools that no pro mixologist would ever leave home without.

Cocktail Shaker. A must-have for mixing really cold, well-shaken cocktails. Always shake vigorously and at least as long as a slow count to ten. Bonus points for shaking to the beat of the music.

Corkscrew. Ever been stuck with a great bottle of wine and no corkscrew? Pure torture, I tell you. I like using the more old-school waiter's corkscrew, which includes a blade and folds up like a pocketknife, but if some of the more fancy options on the market now float your boat, by all means use those instead.

Ice Bucket and Ice Scoop. A really chic addition to break out when preparing drinks on the rocks. I much prefer scoops to tongs, which can get endlessly frustrating by serving up only one cube at a time.

Cutting Board and Knife. For lemons, limes, and other garnishes.

Shot Glass. A shot glass holds 1½ ounces of liquid, so it's a great tool to have on hand when measuring quantities into a cocktail shaker.

Bar Towels. Always have a couple on hand for cleaning up the inevitable spills or splashes.

Pitchers. I collect pretty glass pitchers that I use for mixing up drinks in larger batches as well as for decanting juices and mixers. They look so much prettier placed on the bar than the bottles they came in!

THE ALCOHOL

It's a good idea to keep a full bottle of each of these in the liquor cabinet. Be sure to stock up on more for a party, especially if one of them is an ingredient in your specialty cocktail!

Vodka. I like to keep mine in the freezer so it's always perfectly chilled and ready to go. Vodka is the key ingredient in Bloody Marys, Cosmos, and morning-appropriate Screwdrivers.

Gin. I love the refreshing cucumber flavor of Hendrick's. And nothing's more dangerously delicious than a gimlet made by adding lime juice and soda to a shot of gin!

Rum. Necessary for those days when you're longing to be transported to a Caribbean beach but have to settle for an umbrella-topped drink in your own backyard. I love to use rum in punches, which are a great choice for large parties, since they feel delightfully retro, serve tons of people, and can be mixed completely in advance.

Bourbon. Although I've never personally been a bourbon drinker, having a selection on hand ensures you'll be able to mix up classic cocktails like an old-fashioned. And something about it feels very southern gentleman, don't you think? Wild Turkey is a good and affordable brand.

Tequila. Especially here in Austin (where fiestas are common occurrences), no bar is fully stocked without a bottle of tequila. I like to keep a top-shelf bottle of silver tequila (such as Patrón) that's as great for serving straight up as it is for mixing up a batch of my Watermelon Margaritas (page 267).

Of course, don't forget to heed the most important rule when stocking your bar: make sure you include items that you really enjoy! Your bar is a great way to convey your personal taste, and the items you choose to stock it with can make for really interesting conversation starters.

STRAIGHT FROM THE BOTTLE

As much as I enjoy a great cocktail, my beverage of choice at parties (and with dinner at home!) is typically a glass of crisp white wine. It pairs beautifully with food and perfectly conveys the elegant simplicity I'm always hoping to create at gatherings. Bottom line is—whether you prefer wine or beer—sometimes popping open a bottle and simply *pouring* is all that's needed to get the party started.

WINE

Although I love to drink wine, I'm certainly no connoisseur, and you probably won't find me dwelling on whether a bottle has oaky notes or minerality . . . I'm in it for the pure enjoyment! My father-in-law, who's been in the beverage industry for over forty years and has traveled to the best wineries all over the world, has always taught me that the most important rule when it comes to choosing wine is this: just drink what you like!

With that being said, it can be helpful to have a basic understanding of some of the main types of wine and the foods they generally complement. This merely scratches the surface of some of the great varietals out there, but here's a basic breakdown for some of my favorite wines and when to serve them.

WHITE

Chardonnay. Look for California Chardonnays, which tend to be on the more full-bodied spectrum of whites. Serve with pasta dishes, roast chicken, and richer seafood dishes, such as salmon and scallops.

Pinot Grigio. My personal favorite, Pinot Grigio (often from Italy), is an easy-to-drink wine that's typically fruity and light. Serve with shellfish, frittatas, and in my book, just about anything.

Sauvignon Blanc. One of the crispest and most refreshing whites, Sauvignon Blanc is perfect for hot summer days. It often has herbal or grapefruit notes, with a distinct minerality. Perfect served with grilled fish, mussels, and goat cheese.

RED

Cabernet Sauvignon. A lush red that often tastes of black currant and berries. Look for Cabs from Napa Valley and Bordeaux, and serve with lamb or just about any red meat. A surefire way to fancy up a "burgers on the grill" night!

Pinot Noir. Not quite as bold as a Cab, with layers of softer fruit and an earthy quality. Since it's a bit more delicate, Pinot Noir breaks the "serve white with fish" rule; it's delicious paired with salmon. It's also great with veal and lamb dishes.

Zinfandel. My favorite Zinfandels from Napa Valley taste like cherries and black plums. So delicious served with smoked meats and a wide range of cheeses.

BUBBLY

A bottle of sparkling wine turns an average weeknight into an evening to remember, and a gathering into an all-out celebration. I love the crisp taste of bubbles that pretty much guarantee a good time will be had by all, and I always have a couple of bottles on hand just in case the occasion arises. I usually keep a more moderately priced Prosecco or California sparkling wine in my fridge for casual drinking, as well as a really nice bottle of Champagne for those special occasions when nothing else will do.

For a party, I love to line the rims of Champagne flutes with sparkling sugar and then drop in a couple of berries or pomegranate seeds before filling them up with bubbly for an instant couldn't-be-easier cocktail.

BEER

I make it a rule to always have two cases of beer on hand for backyard barbecues or friends who pop by for impromptu weekend get-togethers. To please a variety of palates, consider keeping an India pale ale (IPA) on hand, which tends to be bitter, floral, and full of hops, as well as a more delicate and less bitter wheat beer. Of course, it's important to know your friends and what they like to drink. If my husband is at a party where they're serving up Miller Lites, he's a happy camper.

THE MIXERS

Mixers and garnishes offer a great opportunity to infuse some personal style into the bar, adding that bit of extra "oomph" that makes basic cocktails feel really festive. I love to get creative with cocktail garnishes and unexpected flavor combinations, as well as fun garnishes that add a bit of a "wow" factor. Here are the basics that I always keep on hand, as well as a few optional extras that are just plain fun.

THE BASICS

Flat and sparkling water, diet and regular soda, tonic water, club soda, orange juice, cranberry juice, lemons, and limes.

THE EXTRAS

Grapefruit Juice. Fresh-squeezed juice is well worth it, and guests will love being offered a Greyhound or Paloma cocktail.

Sparkling Sugar. So elegant lining the rim of a Champagne flute.

Bitters. Aromatics made from herbs and roots. They add complexity to a cocktail and come in loads of interesting flavors, though if I had to choose the one I use most often, orange would definitely win.

Tomato Juice and Bloody Mary Mix. Great for when I don't have time to make my own and a brunch crowd awaits!

Kosher Salt. A must-have for lining the rims of margarita glasses.

Italian Sodas. These fizzy drinks come in a variety of fruity flavors, and I love to keep them on hand to mix with vodka for an instant cocktail. They're also great for offering to guests as a festive nonalcoholic option.

Pineapple Juice. Two words: piña coladas!

Coffee. Why not spike with a bit of Baileys and add some half-and-half for a luxurious after-dinner treat?

THE GLASSWARE

Stock up on a few styles of glassware that you love and you'll be covered for just about any drink situation.

All-Purpose Glass. When I worked in catering, one of my favorite parties that I planned was the grand opening of Austin's Neiman Marcus store. It was a swanky black-tie affair for one thousand guests, and I got to collaborate with Neiman's legendary director of events, Sandy Marple. Miss Marple taught me the value of the all-purpose glass: one that you can use for red and white wine, water, lemonade, spiked punch, and cocktails. It simplifies things for mega-parties like that one, as well as dinner parties at my house, since it means not having to wash four different kinds of glasses at the end of the night. Look for an all-purpose glass that holds about 11 ounces.

Champagne Flute. The narrow mouth keeps the bubbles in your bubbly, and the mere shape of the glass reads instant celebration.

Highball Glass. Serve almost any type of cocktail, beer, and soda in this taller glass.

Old-Fashioned or "Rocks" Glass. This is a shorter glass that's great for any drink served on the rocks.

Martini Glass. This one's a must-have if you think you might be mixing up martinis or Cosmos—they just wouldn't be the same served in anything else!

PARTY QUANTITIES

So your bar is stocked for everyday occasions . . . but how much of everything should you pick up for a bigger shindig? Repeat after me: you do *not* need to offer a million options for every party. For casual gatherings, I tend to keep things really simple by serving beer; white wine; and one fun cocktail, like a margarita. Just make sure to mix up that specialty cocktail in large quantities—it's sure to be a hit!

For larger parties and special occasions, I might add a couple more cocktail choices as well as red wine and Champagne to the mix. And it's always good to have at least a bottle or two of each type of basic alcohol listed in "The Alcohol" (page 258). If one of your friends is a die-hard bourbon fan, you can serve him one on the rocks like a true hostess with the mostest.

Here are a few good rules of thumb that will help you determine how much to buy.

1 | *Plan on pouring one drink per hour per guest. (So for a three-hour party with twenty guests, that's a total of sixty drinks.)*

2 | *The breakdown of how many of each drink gets a little more foggy, since it totally depends on your guests' preferences. My friends tend to like wine, so I usually plan on serving about 40 percent specialty cocktails, 40 percent wine, and 20 percent beer. But if you'll be serving a more beer-friendly crowd, you'd want to increase the amount of beer you'll plan to serve and decrease the amount of wine. In my experience, women drink more specialty cocktails than men. Your best tool here is to get friendly with the staff at your local wine store. They'll be able to provide great recommendations and even food-pairing tips. When in doubt, always buy a little more alcohol than you think you'll need—most liquor stores let you return whatever is unopened after the party.*

3 | *Once you've determined the number of drinks you're planning to serve, it's time to do a little math to determine how many bottles you should purchase to meet that number. Here's your cheat sheet.*
   A 750 ml bottle of wine pours 5 glasses.
   A 750 ml bottle of spirits makes 16 cocktails.

4 | *Beer is easy—I usually let guests drink straight from the bottle. I've found that most beer drinkers prefer this route, and it can drastically cut down on the number of glasses I'm left washing at the end of the night.*

5 | *Don't forget the ice! I always plan on 2 pounds of ice per guest. Buy more if you're planning to ice down beverages in tubs filled with ice.*

6 | *Make sure there's enough glassware. Even though I plan on 1 drink per hour per guest, most guests will refill their wineglasses rather than picking up a clean one with each pour. So, it's usually a safe bet to plan on 2 total glasses per person for the entire party.*

34

BOTTOMS UP!

>>>>>>>>> A FEW SUMMER COCKTAILS <<<<<<<<<

I lived in New York City for a few hot summer months at the end of college, and some of my favorite memories involve meeting friends for brunch at the tapas restaurant around the corner from my SoHo apartment and ordering the signature pitchers of cold fruit-filled sangria that always signified the beginning of the weekend. There's just something about cocktail hour that embodies the footloose and fancy-free vibe of summer—a much-needed reminder that e-mail and to-do lists can wait, and that there's no better way to embrace the moment than relaxing with great conversation and a cold, delicious drink in hand.

Camille

HIBISCUS TEA FIZZ

This drink is my twist on classic iced tea—the ultimate symbol of hospitality in my home state of Texas. The hibiscus flavor of the tea adds an elegant floral note, and the Champagne makes it a party.

MAKES 8 DRINKS

1 cup vodka

2 hibiscus-flavored tea bags

24 fresh blackberries

½ cup honey

1 750 ml bottle sparkling wine, such as Champagne or Prosecco

In a pitcher, combine the vodka and tea bags. Let stand at room temperature for 2 hours and then discard the tea bags. Refrigerate the tea-infused vodka until cold.

In a cocktail shaker, muddle 2 blackberries with 1 or 2 teaspoons honey (make it more or less sweet based on your preference). Add 1 ounce tea-infused vodka and 1 teaspoon cold water and shake vigorously for 30 seconds.

Strain into a Champagne flute, filling each glass to the halfway mark, and then fill the remainder of the flute with Champagne. Garnish with a blackberry and serve. Repeat to make the other drinks.

ROSÉ AND PEACH SANGRIA

Sangria is the go-to drink for savvy hostesses
everywhere: mix up a huge batch the night
before and then chill it and forget it while the
fruit infuses everything with sweetness and
flavor that gets even more delicious the longer
it soaks. In this version, I traded red wine for
a summery rosé and replaced the traditional
brandy with elderflower-scented St-Germain.

MAKES 6 TO 8 DRINKS

½ cup sugar

1 750 ml bottle rosé wine

1 cup St-Germain

2 peaches, pitted and peeled, each sliced into 12
wedges

1 plum, pitted, peeled, and sliced into 8 wedges

¼ cup fresh basil leaves

To make a simple syrup, in a small saucepan bring
the sugar and ½ cup water to a simmer over low heat.
Simmer until the sugar is dissolved and then transfer
to a large pitcher and refrigerate until cold.

To the pitcher, add the wine, St-Germain,
sliced peaches and plum, and basil. Refrigerate
for at least 2 hours and up to overnight. Serve
over ice in a white wine or highball glass.

SPIKED CUCUMBER LIMEADE

It doesn't get more refreshing than this. Tart lime juice, zippy cucumber, and fresh mint come together for a flavor that tastes almost spa-like . . . though a healthy amount of gin ensures that proper festivity will ensue.

MAKES 6 DRINKS

1 cup sugar

1½ cups fresh-squeezed lime juice

½ cup thinly sliced cucumber, plus 6 slices for garnish

8 fresh mint sprigs, plus 6 for garnish

1 cup cucumber-flavored gin, such as Hendrick's

Club soda (optional)

To make a simple syrup, in a small saucepan, bring the sugar and ½ cup water to a simmer over low heat. Simmer until the sugar is dissolved and then transfer to a large pitcher and refrigerate until cold.

Add 1½ cups cold water, the lime juice, the ½ cup of cucumber, the mint, and lots of ice to the pitcher. Stir to combine, then refrigerate for at least 2 hours or overnight.

Add the gin and stir well. Fill 6 glasses with crushed ice, pour the limeade into highball glasses, and garnish each with a cucumber slice and mint sprig. If club soda is desired, fill the glass only three-quarters full with limeade and top off with club soda.

WATERMELON MARGARITAS

In my book, the only thing better than a classic margarita is one that's dialed up with fresh watermelon juice: summer in a glass! This one is such a crowd-pleaser that it just might be destined to become your new signature drink of summer. Go ahead and take all the credit—I won't tell.

MAKES 6 DRINKS

6 cups seedless watermelon, cut into chunks

½ cup light agave nectar

½ cup lime juice

1½ cups silver tequila

1 lime wedge, plus lime wheels for garnish

Kosher salt

In a blender, puree the watermelon until smooth. Place a fine-mesh strainer over a large bowl and strain the watermelon juice. Transfer the juice to a large pitcher. Add the agave nectar, lime juice, and tequila. Stir well and then refrigerate until cold.

Use the lime wedge to moisten the outer rim of 6 glasses and then twist the edge of each glass into a saucer full of kosher salt. Fill the glasses with ice and then pour the margarita over it. Garnish each with a lime wheel and serve.

35

ALFRESCO ANNIVERSARY DINNER

Several years ago, I read an article in a travel magazine about Capri—its breathtaking views of the Mediterranean, charming streets lined with bougainvillea-covered buildings, and the Hollywood stars who vacationed there (Grace Kelly, Liz Taylor, and Sophia Loren, to name a few), which solidified its long-held reputation as a playground for the rich and famous. Flash-forward several years: Adam and I had just gotten engaged, and as we started planning our honeymoon destination, my mind wandered back to that article and my lifelong dream of setting foot on Capri myself. Our tickets were booked.

We spent two magical weeks on the island, completely unplugged from technology and spending our days eating gelato in the piazza and our nights sipping limoncello and watching the crashing waves from the balcony of our cliff-hanging hotel. I was enchanted by the otherworldly beauty of the island from the moment I laid eyes on it; the salty air itself seemed to carry the promise of a perfect day that couldn't be repeated anywhere else.

One day, we chartered a speedboat and were whisked away by our Italian tour guide (young, tan, and shirtless, which seemed to be de rigueur among the locals) to a few of the surrounding islands. We stopped off at Positano, where we devoured the freshest grilled fish served with a lemony pasta, sipped glasses of Prosecco, and then explored the town square where we stumbled upon an in-progress wedding that looked straight out of a fairy tale. I pinched myself as we watched the beautiful young bride descend the stairs of a tiny village cathedral, her family and neighbors cheering and singing.

Camille

Another day was spent wandering the shops in Capri town, trying on dresses I couldn't afford in the legendary Missoni boutique, stocking up on gifts to take back to family at Capri's famous perfumery, and of course, being fitted for my own pair of classic leather Capri sandals by a local craftsman. I felt as glamorous as Jackie O as we stopped off for a long lunch and watched the tourists passing by at a charming cafe in the piazza.

It's been four years since that unforgettable trip, and for this year's wedding anniversary, I decided to channel its magic by creating a Capri-inspired dinner by the pool for us to enjoy together. I draped the table with an azure-striped linen and filled a big wooden bowl with lemons that immediately recalled the night we dined at tables under a lemon grove. A couple pots of herbs filled the air with the delicious scents of rosemary bushes and olive trees that line the streets of Capri.

As we polished off the last bite of berries with ricotta cream, we raised a glass of Prosecco to four great years of marriage that somehow *flew* by. For a while, I forgot about work deadlines and loads of laundry and felt almost as if I were on the terrace of our hotel in Capri gazing out at the Mediterranean. Maybe the view wasn't quite the same, but four years later, the company was even better.

The MENU

If there's one thing I'll always associate with Capri, it's the unmatched flavor combination of sweet tomatoes, fresh basil, and the creamiest mozzarella I've ever tasted. The famous Caprese salad was born on the island, after all, so when we were there we threw caution to the wind and gave in to the temptation to eat some form of the triumvirate at just about every meal: Caprese salads with just-caught tuna for lunch, a ball of buffalo mozzarella drizzled with olive oil and served with bread for a cocktail-hour treat, and the freshest gnocchi tossed with barely cooked tomatoes and basil for dinner. We couldn't get enough, and when creating the menu for our anniversary dinner, I knew I wanted to let those three ingredients play starring roles in each course.

TO DRINK	HORS D'OEUVRES ON THE PATIO	FIRST COURSE	SOMETHING SWEET
PROSECCO ON ICE WITH MINT, RASPBERRIES, BLACKBERRIES, AND LIME, PAGE 275	ANTIPASTO SPREAD WITH PROSCIUTTO, HOMEMADE RICOTTA (PAGE 276), CERIGNOLA OLIVES, FRESH FIGS, ORANGE BLOSSOM HONEY, AND CROSTINI (PAGE 177)	CAPRESE BUCATINI, PAGE 277	BERRIES WITH RICOTTA CREAM, PAGE 281
		SECOND COURSE	
		GRILLED HALIBUT WITH HEIRLOOM TOMATOES, PAGE 279	

GET THE LOOK

For a romantic dinner at home, think about what little touches will elevate the experience beyond your usual suppertime setup. I chose a color palette of Mediterranean blue, lemon, and olive that recalled the shades of our Capri honeymoon. Instead of a floral arrangement, I kept things rustic and natural by using edible elements as the table centerpiece. Baskets of crusty bread, beautiful blocks of Parmesan ready for grating, and olive oil decanted into a pretty glass bottle are staples at every cafe in Italy, and they added charm to our dinner table in Austin. I included a couple pots of herbs (which got planted in our garden the next day!) and a wooden bowl overflowing with lemons for a cheerful pop of yellow.

Consider bringing a few pieces of your indoor furniture outdoors for the evening. I pulled a pair of lounge-y chairs from our bedroom out onto the patio to make a comfy spot for us to enjoy pre-dinner Prosecco. It's a surprising touch that creates an instantly festive vibe.

WHEN LIFE GIVES YOU LEMONS

Capri is famous for its beautiful lemon groves, and one of my favorite memories from our trip was the night we dined under a canopy of lemon trees at the famed Ristorante da Paolino. Though I couldn't cast quite the same spell over our dinner, I gave a nod to that night by filling a large wood bowl with beautiful and fragrant lemons and then tucked in a few lemon leaves to fill any gaps. I pruned branches from the lemon tree in our backyard, but you can also order the foliage from any local flower market. When purchasing lemons at the grocery store or farmers' market, it pays to be picky: make sure you use the largest, heaviest, most unblemished fruit you can find.

ARRANGE THE PERFECT ANTIPASTO

Antipasto—an appetizer consisting of meats, cheeses, olives, and more—is practically an art form in Italy. There are so many great combinations possible, and I love the opportunity to get creative with different flavors and experiment with finding the best pairings. Since antipasto is typically served very simply, this is the time to seek out the highest quality of ingredients and let the individual flavors really shine.

I love to display antipasto on a big rustic wood cutting board—the variety of colors and textures makes for such a beautiful presentation that it practically begs guests to gather around the table. Don't worry too much about making everything look perfect—this is really the cook's opportunity to experiment and have some fun. For guests, it's a chance to indulge and savor interesting flavors—and awaken the palate for the rest of the meal.

When planning my antipasto, I always aim to include a mix of contrasting flavors and textures. Fresh figs taste even sweeter next to salty prosciutto, funky blue cheese balances the floral notes in honey, and meaty Cerignola olives taste great with, well, just about everything. It's really all about taking your guests on a flavor adventure where they can try something new and open up their senses for the feast that awaits.

A LITTLE LOVE NOTE

An anniversary is the perfect time to pen a few words of affection. In keeping with our Capri getaway theme, I ordered a pair of vintage postcards online and we wrote notes to each other, which I then placed at each of our settings at the table. After dinner, I added mine to the drawer where I keep all the other letters and cards that Adam has given me through the years—a sweet memory to reread for many anniversaries to come.

COOKING AS A COUPLE

On normal weeknights at our house, I'm usually the cook, so when Adam and I head into the kitchen to prepare a meal together, it feels really special. I've learned that it works well for each person to have one menu item that they can "own" and totally oversee from start to finish. The other person can play the part of sous-chef and take instructions, but ultimately each person can feel responsible for one aspect of the meal and then take all the credit for how delicious it turns out. It also solves any potential disagreements if either partner tends to be a bit bossy in the kitchen: when Adam's the lead on a dish, he calls the shots, and vice versa!

Above all, realize that the preparation can be as romantic as the meal itself—there's no need to rush through each step! Slow down, open a bottle of wine, turn on some great music, and savor the process of cooking together.

bottoms up!

One night in Capri, we headed to the iconic Grand Hotel Quisisana—everyone from Ernest Hemingway to Tom Cruise has stayed there—for an unforgettable dinner on its beautiful terrace. But first, we couldn't pass up the Quisisana's cocktail-hour tradition: a bottle of Champagne on ice, glasses garnished with mint, raspberries, blackberries, and lime slices. It was such a completely festive start to the evening that it was a must for our at-home dinner date.

This one is really all about the presentation: I pulled out a rustic ceramic wine bucket to hold our bubbly (I went with Prosecco, the Italian version of Champagne) on ice while we lounged on the patio and then set out little bowls with all the colorful garnishes that looked so pretty next to our Champagne glasses. A cocktail recipe really doesn't get simpler than this—and it's an undeniably romantic way to kick off the evening.

HOMEMADE RICOTTA

This recipe might just become a game-changer for you. Homemade ricotta falls into that category of items (along with homemade bread and fresh pasta) that sound really impressive but are actually so easy when you've mastered the simple technique. And once you taste the addictively creamy cheese that this recipe yields, you'll never go back to the store-bought stuff. I'm constantly trying to think of new ways to use it: topping crostini with grilled peaches, tossed into a pasta with summer vegetables, and of course, served as the centerpiece of an antipasto spread as I did here.

MAKES 2 CUPS

6 cups whole milk

¾ cup heavy whipping cream

½ teaspoon kosher salt

3 tablespoons fresh lemon juice

Line a fine-mesh sieve with two layers of cheesecloth. Place the sieve over a large bowl.

In a heavy pot over medium heat, bring the milk, cream, and salt to a boil, stirring frequently. Reduce heat to low, add the lemon juice, and let simmer, stirring constantly. When the mixture begins to curdle (about 3 minutes), remove from the heat.

Pour the mixture into the cheesecloth-lined sieve and let it drain completely (this takes about 45 minutes). Discard the liquid and refrigerate the ricotta in a covered container. Store in the fridge for up to 4 days.

BITS OF BRILLIANCE:

In Capri, I became obsessed with the ubiquitous buffalo mozzarella that was made fresh, right on the island. Italy is known for having some of the best dairy water buffaloes in the world, and the decadently creamy cheese they produce is truly unlike anything I've experienced in America. I've tried a few different brands of buffalo mozzarella imported from Italy, and the time required to transport makes a perceptible difference in the texture of the cheese. I've found that the very best mozzarella currently available in America is handcrafted from cow's milk and produced in small batches. Look for it to be made in the last couple of days, as the height of freshness really makes all the difference.

CAPRESE BUCATINI

We ate some form of this pasta almost daily when we were in Capri: the combination of fresh tomatoes, creamy mozzarella, and basil is unmatched. Look for bucatini at specialty pasta stores—it's a thicker noodle that's hollow in the middle, perfect for sopping up every last bit of flavor. Spaghetti works great, too.

SERVES 2 TO 3

2 tablespoons extra-virgin olive oil, plus more for finishing

1 shallot, diced

2 garlic cloves, minced

Splash of dry white wine

1½ cups cherry tomatoes, halved

½ pound bucatini, spaghetti, or linguine

½ cup fresh basil leaves, torn by hand, plus more for garnish

Kosher salt and freshly ground black pepper

1 8-ounce ball fresh mozzarella, torn by hand

Bring a large pot of salted water to a boil.

In a large skillet, heat the oil over medium heat. Add the shallot and cook for 3 minutes, just until soft. Add the garlic and cook for 1 minute more. Add the dry white wine and bring to a simmer and then add the tomatoes and turn off the heat. You don't want them to cook—only to warm through gently.

Meanwhile, add the bucatini to the pot and cook until al dente, according to the package directions. Use a pasta server to scoop the pasta from the pot to the skillet with the tomato mixture—a little of the pasta water will transfer into the skillet, helping the sauce to coat the pasta. Add the basil to the skillet, season with salt and pepper, and gently toss it all together until combined.

Divide the pasta between 2 or 3 bowls and then top with the torn mozzarella. Drizzle a bit of olive oil over the top and garnish with fresh basil.

Make the most of summer tomatoes! When choosing them at the market, select tomatoes that are firm, with just a little give when gently pressed. They should be brilliantly colored, unwrinkled, and have a sweet, woody smell. When you get them home, store unwrapped at room temperature (never in the fridge!). They're undeniably delicious lightly cooked as in this dish, but nothing beats the simple pleasure of sliced ripe tomatoes drizzled with a touch of extra-virgin olive oil and a sprinkle of flaky sea salt.

GRILLED HALIBUT WITH HEIRLOOM TOMATOES

Some of my most memorable meals from our honeymoon took place at the charming, no-frills cafes that dot the coastline, serving up the best of the day's catch. This dish could easily be found on one of their menus: delicately flavored halibut seasoned simply with just a drizzle of extra-virgin olive oil, lots of fresh-squeezed lemon, and sea salt, and served over a bed of barely cooked heirloom tomatoes.

SERVES 2

HEIRLOOM TOMATO MIXTURE

2 tablespoons extra-virgin olive oil

1 large shallot, minced

1 tablespoon chopped garlic

¼ cup dry white wine

2 cups mixed heirloom tomatoes, cut into wedges

10 black olives, pitted

½ cup fresh basil leaves, plus more for garnish

Kosher salt and freshly ground black pepper

HALIBUT

2 5-ounce halibut fillets, about 1 inch thick

Extra-virgin olive oil

Juice and zest of 1 lemon

Kosher salt and freshly ground black pepper

Maldon sea salt

To prepare the tomatoes, in a medium skillet heat the oil over medium heat. Add the shallot and sauté until it begins to become golden, about 5 minutes. Add the garlic and cook for 1 minute. Add the wine and bring to a simmer and then add the tomatoes and olives and cook for 2 minutes, until the tomatoes are just warmed through. Tear the basil by hand and add to the mixture. Liberally season with salt and pepper.

To prepare the fish, heat a grill to medium-high heat. Drizzle the halibut with oil and sprinkle the lemon juice and zest on both sides. Season on both sides with kosher salt and pepper. Grill 3 to 4 minutes on each side, until the fish flakes easily with a fork.

Spoon half the tomato mixture onto each of 2 plates and top with a grilled halibut fillet, a sprinkle of Maldon salt, and 1 or 2 fresh basil leaves.

BERRIES WITH RICOTTA CREAM

Though most people associate ricotta with savory dishes, its mild and lightly sweet flavor lends itself amazingly well to desserts. This vanilla-bean-flecked ricotta cream is one of my favorite sweets in the world: I can hardly keep myself from licking every last beater and spatula clean when I whip it up.

SERVES 2

⅓ cup heavy whipping cream

¼ cup Homemade Ricotta (page 276) or store-bought whole-milk ricotta cheese

Seeds from 1 vanilla bean pod

1 tablespoon confectioners' sugar

1 teaspoon grated lemon zest

1 cup fresh blueberries

1 cup fresh raspberries

1 cup fresh strawberries, hulled and quartered

1 tablespoon granulated sugar

4 amaretto cookies or Chocolate-Dipped Cherry Almond Biscotti (page 153)

2 fresh mint sprigs, for garnish

In a small bowl, stir 1 tablespoon of the cream into the ricotta. In the bowl of an electric mixer fitted with the whisk attachment, beat the remaining cream with the vanilla bean seeds, confectioners' sugar, and lemon zest until semifirm peaks form. Fold the ricotta into the whipped cream mixture and then refrigerate until ready to use.

In a medium bowl, combine the berries and the granulated sugar. Stir to combine and then chill in the refrigerator for at least 15 minutes or up to 2 hours to let macerate. Divide the berries between 2 compote dishes and top with the ricotta cream. Crumble the cookies over the top, garnish each dish with the mint, and serve.

36

PIZZA GRILLING PARTY

I think every host should have one signature meal that he or she feels supremely confident preparing, one that will garner oohs and aahs and leave friends begging for the recipe. If I had to choose, grilled pizza could definitely be considered my signature, and I'd be as excited to serve it to the president (if he happened to stop by) as I would to good friends at a laid-back summertime gathering.

You could call me a bit of a pizza connoisseur, always on the hunt for that elusive crispy-on-the-outside, chewy-on-the-inside crust, topped with inventive seasonal ingredients and really great fresh mozzarella. When traveling, I seek out the best pizzas wherever I go, debating their merits and weaknesses and always taking notes on interesting topping combinations to bring back home. My favorite pizzas in the world? Gjelina in Venice Beach, California, Pizza Chic in Paris (who knew that Paris would have amazing pizza!), and this little spot in Rome that I'm not sure I'll ever be able to find again—though I'd happily go back to Italy just to hunt for it! And really, who in their right mind *doesn't* love pizza? A really great one with the perfect balance of flavors can be a transporting experience, and I've spent many nights testing and perfecting a handful of my very favorite varieties to pull out for dinner parties.

Although my obsession with pizza goes way back, it wasn't until I attended a "culinary boot camp" a few years ago at the Culinary Institute of America in Napa Valley that I learned the secret to making the best pizza at home. While there, I was lucky enough to have Chef John Ash as my instructor, and one day in class he taught us how to make the perfect dough (no kneading required!) and then use a simple but exacting technique for cooking pizzas on the grill. One bite and I knew I'd discovered something very special, and I've been making this pizza on a near-weekly basis ever since.

Camille

The thing about pizzas is they're much more fun to make and eat with a group. Some of my very favorite dinner party memories revolve around inviting a bunch of friends to join us around the grill, everyone weighing in on their favorite topping combinations. I give each person a specific task to perform: a couple of guests might be brushing the raw dough with olive oil while others are throwing toppings onto the pizza mid-grill, and someone else is slicing into a perfectly charred pie that's ready to eat! When we all gather around the table, everyone gets to enjoy the fruits of their labor, savoring the satisfaction of preparing a meal together.

For this late-summer gathering, I invited four good friends to join Adam and me at dusk to cook and eat a few of our favorite pies on the patio. We poured wine (the first step to any great interactive cooking experience!) and set out a few snacks to nibble on while we got to work. I rolled out the dough and enlisted the help of Sarah and Ana to do some final prep, like chopping herbs and gathering toppings to take out to the grill. I'd taken care of most of the toppings the night before to keep things fuss-free the day of the party. Meanwhile, the guys headed to the backyard to hang out while Adam prepared the two-sided grill (more on that later).

As we sat around the table feasting on pizzas set out on cutting boards, I couldn't help but think that these kinds of nights are what summer entertaining is all about: making simple food with great friends with nowhere else we need to be and then pouring the wine and hanging out long past sunset.

The
MENU
PIZZA GRILLING PARTY

I prepped a variety of great toppings so that guests can build their own pizzas, but I always have a few great topping combinations in mind that never fail to be showstoppers. This menu includes my very favorites plus a couple of simple sides that can be completely prepared before guests arrive. Dessert couldn't be simpler: high-quality vanilla gelato with just-brewed espresso poured over the top. Simplicity at its very best.

APPETIZERS	THE PIZZAS	ON THE SIDE	FOR DESSERT
FARMERS' MARKET CRUDITÉS WITH BASIL PESTO, PAGE 291	CARAMELIZED ONION AND PROSCIUTTO PIZZA, PAGE 297 BUTTERNUT AND BLUE CHEESE PIZZA, PAGE 298 MARGHERITA PIZZA WITH FRIED SAGE, PAGE 299 WILD MUSHROOM AND RICOTTA PIZZA, PAGE 301 FIG AND GOAT CHEESE PIZZA, PAGE 301	BEET AND AVOCADO SALAD WITH ORANGE VINAIGRETTE, PAGE 302 PARMESAN-ROASTED CAULIFLOWER WITH GOLDEN RAISINS AND PINE NUTS, PAGE 303	*AFFOGATO*, PAGE 304

GET THE LOOK

Pizza nights call for a simple, organic table setting that lets the vibrant pizzas play a starring role in the center of the table. A linen runner lets the beauty of a rustic wood table show through, and striped napkins, stemless wine tumblers, and sturdy enamelware plates stay within the modern and neutral palette.

In the center of the table, I placed a couple pots of herbs that echo the flavors in each pizza. There's something about herbs that transport me to an Italian cafe; plus, in the middle of summer, they're one of the only living centerpieces that won't wilt in the heat! Make sure to leave room for the pizzas, since after they come off the grill they'll be placed on big wood cutting boards and added to the tabletop mix.

Since the grill is the central component of this party, I make it colorful by piling up heirloom tomatoes, jars of herbs, and all the bowls of toppings to get everyone excited to start cooking.

LESS IS MORE

One of the most important pizza-making lessons I learned from Chef Ash is that when it comes to toppings, less is definitely more. In Italy, chefs celebrate the simplicity of a great pizza with toppings applied sparingly so as not to cover up the beauty of a perfectly charred crust. The key is using the highest-quality ingredients and the freshest cheese you can get your hands on and then adding them with a light hand so that those beautiful flavors can be truly savored. So, no matter how amazing that fresh ricotta or buffalo mozzarella is, resist the urge to pile it on!

GET ORGANIZED

Hosting a party in which everyone pitches in with the cooking means embracing a little spontaneity, but it also requires being organized from the start. Before guests arrive, spend some time prepping all the toppings. All those little tasks (grating cheese, slicing tomatoes, caramelizing onions) can take a bit more time than anticipated, so I aim to prep in the morning and stash all my little bowls of toppings in the fridge so they're ready to go at party time.

At an interactive-style party, things will go a lot more smoothly if you brainstorm a few specific tasks for guests to do when they arrive. Then set out the items they'll need in advance: place a couple of cutting boards and sharp knives on the counter as well as all the tools necessary for grilling and serving the pizzas. That way, you're not left to answer a bunch of questions or rummage through cabinets when you're hustling to get pizzas onto the grill.

FOR DESSERT, KEEP IT SIMPLE!

Do as the Italians do and serve a simple dessert of sorbet, fresh fruit, or a plate of biscotti with glasses of Vin Santo. After a big meal (at which everyone's eaten way too much pizza, no doubt), the dessert course is really just a way to end the evening on a sweet note. One of my favorite flavor combinations in the world is ice cream and coffee, so when I tried *affogato*—Italian for "drowned"—for the first time at an Italian restaurant a few years ago, I thought I'd died and gone to heaven. It starts with a scoop of rich vanilla gelato that's topped with just-brewed espresso. The interplay of hot-meets-cold and sweet-meets-bitter makes this dish so much more than the sum of its parts. And after an evening spent in the kitchen, you really can't beat a dessert that calls for only two ingredients!

NO GRILL? NO PROB!

Although we're pretty addicted to grilling pizzas at our house, there have been stormy nights when we've been forced to cook inside, so I've perfected an in-oven technique that won't disappoint. The key is to use a pizza stone: allowing it to get extremely hot before sliding the pizza on simulates the effect of placing it on the screaming hot grill. Here's how to do it:

1 | *Place an oven rack in the upper third of the oven, and slide your pizza stone on top. Turn the oven to its hottest setting, at least 500°F, and let the pizza stone heat up for an entire hour (yes, you heard me: don't skip this step!).*

2 | *After rolling out the dough, turn the oven to broil. Sprinkle a pizza peel with flour to prevent the dough from sticking and place the pizza dough onto the peel.*

3 | *Add all your toppings, remembering to use a light hand.*

4 | *Carefully slide the pizza from the peel onto the pizza stone, shaking back and forth a bit to help the pizza slide on. Bake the pizza until the bottom of the crust is very crisp, about 5 minutes (rotate halfway through).*

5 | *Gently slide the pizza back onto the peel and transfer to your cutting board to slice and serve.*

SOURCES

Floral design: The Nouveau Romantics
Food styling: Ann Lowe
Furniture: Loot Vintage Rentals

FAVORS

Send guests home with bottles of handmade infused olive oil to inspire more culinary adventures. I infused mine with oranges and rosemary—perfect as a dipping sauce for bread, brushed onto uncooked pizza dough, or drizzled over roasted vegetables.

FARMERS' MARKET CRUDITÉS WITH BASIL PESTO

In the summertime, when my basil plants are growing so quickly I can't seem to keep up, I make pesto. It requires so much of the herb that I rarely make it at other times of the year, and nothing tastes more like summer than the classic combo of basil, garlic, lemon, and olive oil. Feel free to sub in other herbs and nuts, and if you have extra pesto, freeze single-serve portions in an ice-cube tray and then pop them into freezer storage bags to enjoy year-round.

SERVES 6 AS AN APPETIZER

PESTO

2 cups fresh basil leaves

2 garlic cloves

1 tablespoon pine nuts, plus more for garnish

3 tablespoons Parmigiano-Reggiano

Juice of 1 lemon

⅓ cup extra-virgin olive oil

Kosher salt and freshly ground black pepper

RAW SEASONAL VEGETABLES

6 CUPS

Radishes, cleaned, stems removed, and halved if large

Baby carrots

Asparagus, trimmed and lightly blanched

Yellow bell peppers, cored, seeded, and cut into thin strips

Seedless cucumbers, peeled and sliced on the bias

Radicchio, leaves separated

Maldon sea salt or another flaky salt, for finishing

Prepare a bowl of ice and cold water. In a saucepan of boiling salted water, blanch the basil and garlic for a couple seconds and then transfer them with a slotted spoon to the bowl of ice water to shock them and stop the cooking. Drain and pat dry with a clean kitchen towel.

In a blender or food processor, pulse the basil, garlic, pine nuts, Parmigiano-Reggiano, and lemon juice until combined. With the motor running, slowly stream in the oil until the entire mixture is emulsified. Add a pinch of kosher salt and pepper and combine. Taste and adjust the seasonings as needed.

Transfer to a small serving bowl, top with the reserved pine nuts, and artfully arrange the vegetables around it on a serving platter. Sprinkle the entire platter with a liberal dose of sea salt.

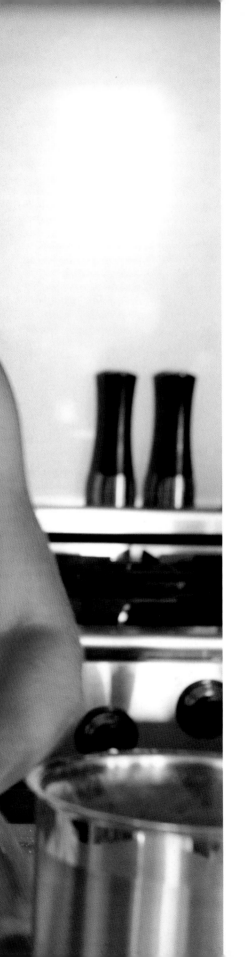

PERFECT PIZZA DOUGH

*MAKES 24 OUNCES OF DOUGH,
ENOUGH FOR SIX 10-INCH CRUSTS*

1 envelope (2.5 teaspoons) active dry yeast

2 cups warm water

2 teaspoons sugar

3 teaspoons kosher salt

½ cup finely ground cornmeal

3 tablespoons olive oil

4½ to 5 cups all-purpose flour

In the bowl of an electric mixer fitted with the dough hook, stir the yeast into the water and sugar. After 5 minutes, it should bubble. When it does, stir in the salt, cornmeal, and 1 tablespoon of the oil.

Add the flour ½ cup at a time, stirring at low speed until the dough forms a ball and pulls away from the sides of the bowl (about 4 minutes). You may need to add a little more flour or water to get the right consistency. Let the dough rest in the bowl for 15 minutes. It should be fairly soft.

Remove the dough from the bowl and divide it into 6 equal pieces. Gently round each piece into a ball and brush with the remaining oil. Place each ball in a zippered plastic storage bag and seal the bags closed. Let sit for at least 30 minutes, or for the best flavor, refrigerate them overnight. Remove from the fridge at least 1 hour before making the pizzas. You can also freeze the dough for up to 3 months—just be sure to let it thaw and come to room temperature before rolling out.

STEPS TO THE PERFECT PIZZA

1 | On a lightly floured cutting board, roll the dough into a 10-inch free-form circle as thinly as you can. Even thinness is key, but don't worry too much about making it perfectly round, oval, or rectangular . . . embrace an irregular rustic look. Place on a sheet pan or cutting board, with sheets of parchment paper layered between stacked crusts.

2 | Completely prep all your ingredients and set them next to the grill beforehand, since once the cooking process starts everything moves very quickly. For an interactive pizza party with a big group of friends, set out tons of ingredients and let guests build their favorite combos. For this party, offerings included caramelized onions, thinly sliced prosciutto, roasted butternut squash, blistered cherry tomatoes, fresh mozzarella, crumbled blue cheese, peppery arugula, and more.

3 | The key to grilling the perfect pizza is all about getting the grill hot, hot, hot! Prepare a two-temperature grill: one side should be at the highest temperature possible (I bring mine up to 600°F) and the other side should be on low heat. Brush one side of a dough round with olive oil, carefully place the oiled side down onto the hottest part of the grill, and close the grill as quickly as possible to prevent as little heat from escaping as possible.

4 | Within a minute, the dough will puff and bubble on top. Lift the edge with tongs or a spatula, and if grill marks are visible, flip the crust over onto the cooler side of the grill.

5 | Starting with your base or sauce, spread a thin layer of all your desired toppings onto the crust, leaving a 1-inch border. Immediately close the grill hood and cook for a few minutes, until the cheese melts. You want to work as quickly as possible, since as soon as you close the grill, you create a flow of convection heat that simulates a pizza oven and results in the perfect crispy crust.

6 | After 3 minutes or so, peek under the hood to check on the pizza—it's done when the cheese is melted.

7 | Using a large spatula, transfer the pizza to a cutting board. Always add herbs or fresh greens after grilling, so they don't wilt. Serve the pizzas family-style on a big wood cutting board in the middle of the table, and cut into squares or wedges with a very sharp pizza wheel.

GARLIC-INFUSED OIL AND BUTTER SAUCE

4 garlic cloves, chopped

½ cup extra-virgin olive oil

4 tablespoons (½ stick) butter, melted

In a small saucepan, bring the garlic and oil to a simmer and then reduce the heat to low and cook for 3 to 5 minutes, until the garlic starts to brown. Turn off the heat and then whisk in the melted butter in a steady stream until combined.

CARAMELIZED ONION AND PROSCIUTTO PIZZA

MAKES ONE 10-INCH PIZZA

1 tablespoon butter

1 white or sweet onion, sliced

1 tablespoon minced fresh thyme

1 teaspoon sugar

½ teaspoon kosher salt

1 4-ounce ball Perfect Pizza Dough (page 293) or store-bought dough, at room temperature

Garlic-Infused Oil and Butter Sauce (opposite)

½ cup grated fresh mozzarella

6 to 8 very thin slices prosciutto

2 cups baby arugula

Extra-virgin olive oil

To caramelize the onion, melt the butter in a large skillet over medium heat. Add the onion and sauté until just tender, about 6 minutes. Add the thyme, reduce the heat to medium-low, and cook until the onion is golden, stirring often, about 20 minutes. Sprinkle the sugar over the onion and sauté 20 more minutes, until the onion is golden brown, reduced, and very sweet. If the pan gets dry, add a little water so that the onion doesn't burn. Set aside to cool (this can be done a day in advance and kept in the refrigerator).

Preheat the grill, one side on high and one side on low. Roll out the dough according to the "Steps to the Perfect Pizza" (page 294). Gather all your toppings (onion, garlic-infused sauce, mozzarella, prosciutto, and arugula), plus your dough and oil, on a large tray, and head out to the grill.

Using my two-temperature grilling technique, grill the first side of the pizza. Flip when ready and then brush the pizza evenly with garlic-infused sauce and top with the caramelized onion and mozzarella. Close the hood, and when the cheese is melted, transfer the pizza to a cutting board.

Top the pizza with the prosciutto and arugula. Cut into wedges and serve.

BUTTERNUT AND BLUE CHEESE PIZZA

MAKES ONE 10-INCH PIZZA

1 butternut squash, neck only, cut into ½-inch cubes

Extra-virgin olive oil

1 tablespoon pure maple syrup

½ teaspoon crushed red pepper flakes

½ teaspoon kosher salt

1 4-ounce ball Perfect Pizza Dough (page 293) or store-bought dough, at room temperature

½ cup grated fresh mozzarella

¼ cup crumbled blue cheese (I love Cambozola)

2 cups baby arugula

Maldon sea salt

Preheat the oven to 450°F and cover a baking sheet with foil (to make cleanup easier).

In a bowl, combine the squash, 1 tablespoon of the oil, the maple syrup, red pepper flakes, and kosher salt and toss to combine. Spread the squash evenly on the foiled baking sheet. Roast for about 30 minutes, until tender and caramelized on the edges, tossing a couple of times during baking. Transfer the squash to a prep bowl.

Preheat the grill. Roll out the dough according to "Steps to the Perfect Pizza" on page 294. Gather all your toppings (squash, mozzarella, blue cheese, and arugula), plus your dough and oil, and head out to the grill. Using my two-temperature grilling technique, grill the first side of the pizza. Flip when ready and then top the crust with the squash and cheeses. Close the hood, and when the cheeses are melted, transfer the pizza to a cutting board.

Top the pizza with the arugula and sprinkle with sea salt. Cut into wedges and serve.

MARGHERITA PIZZA WITH FRIED SAGE

MAKES ONE 10-INCH PIZZA

Extra-virgin olive oil

2 garlic cloves, chopped

1 cup cherry tomatoes, stems removed

Kosher salt and freshly ground black pepper

¼ teaspoon crushed red pepper flakes

Leaves from 1 bunch fresh sage

1 4-ounce ball Perfect Pizza Dough (page 293) or store-bought dough, at room temperature

½ cup grated fresh mozzarella

Maldon sea salt

Heat 1 tablespoon of oil in a medium skillet over medium heat. Add the garlic and sauté for 1 minute. Add the tomatoes, kosher salt and pepper to taste, and the red pepper flakes; increase the heat to high. Sauté until the tomatoes are charred and beginning to break down, 3 to 5 minutes. Transfer to a bowl and then use your hands to gently crush the tomatoes, leaving large chunks intact.

Heat 2 tablespoons of olive oil in a small skillet over high heat. When a drop of water makes it sizzle, you know it's ready. Add only as many sage leaves as can fit in a single layer. Fry for 15 seconds, then use a slotted spoon to flip over. Fry for another 15 seconds and then transfer with a slotted spoon to a paper-towel-lined plate. Repeat with the remaining sage leaves, adding more oil as needed to coat the bottom of the skillet.

Preheat the grill. Roll out the dough according to "Steps to the Perfect Pizza" on page 294. Gather all your toppings (tomato sauce, sage leaves, and mozzarella), plus your dough and oil, and head out to the grill.

Using my two-temperature grilling technique, brush the crust with oil, then grill the first side of the pizza. Flip when ready and then top the crust with an even layer of tomato sauce and mozzarella. Close the hood, and when the cheese is melted, transfer the pizza to a cutting board.

Top the pizza with fried sage leaves and Maldon sea salt to taste. Cut into wedges and serve.

FIG AND GOAT CHEESE PIZZA

1 4-ounce ball Perfect Pizza Dough (page 293) or store-bought dough, at room temperature

Extra-virgin olive oil

10 fresh figs, halved or quartered

½ cup grated fresh mozzarella

¼ cup crumbled goat cheese

½ cup fresh mint leaves

⅓ cup toasted walnuts, roughly chopped (see page 47)

Maldon sea salt

Preheat the grill. Roll out the dough according to "Steps to the Perfect Pizza" on page 294. Gather all your toppings (figs, mozzarella, and goat cheese), plus your dough and oil, and head out to the grill. Using my two-temperature grilling technique, grill the first side of the pizza. Flip when ready and then top the crust with the figs and cheeses. Close the hood, and when the cheeses are melted, transfer the pizza to a cutting board.

Top the pizza with the mint, walnuts, and a sprinkle of Maldon salt. Cut into wedges and serve.

WILD MUSHROOM AND RICOTTA PIZZA

2 tablespoons butter

1 shallot, thinly sliced

1 pound assorted wild mushrooms (cremini, oyster, chanterelle, shiitake . . . whatever you have will work just fine!)

2 garlic cloves, chopped

2 teaspoons chopped fresh rosemary

Kosher salt and freshly ground black pepper

½ cup dry white wine

1 4-ounce ball Perfect Pizza Dough (page 293) or store-bought dough, at room temperature

Extra-virgin olive oil

Garlic-Infused Oil and Butter Sauce (page 296)

½ cup Homemade Ricotta (page 276) or store-bought whole-milk ricotta, at room temperature

2 cups baby arugula

Melt the butter in a medium skillet over medium-high heat. Add the shallot and sauté for a couple of minutes, until it starts to soften. Add the mushrooms, garlic, and rosemary, season with salt and pepper, and sauté for 3 minutes, or until mushrooms start to brown. Add the wine and simmer, stirring frequently, until all the liquid has cooked off and the mushrooms are golden brown, 10 to 12 minutes. Set aside to cool. (The mushroom mixture can be made a day in advance and kept in the refrigerator.)

Preheat the grill. Roll out the dough according to "Steps to the Perfect Pizza" on page 294. Gather all your toppings (mushrooms, garlic-infused sauce, ricotta, and arugula), plus your dough and oil, and head out to the grill.

Using my two-temperature grilling technique, grill the first side of the pizza. Flip when ready and then brush the pizza evenly with garlic-infused sauce and top with the mushrooms and ricotta. Close the hood, and when the cheese is melted, transfer the pizza to a cutting board.

Top the pizza with arugula. Cut into wedges and serve.

BEET AND AVOCADO SALAD WITH ORANGE VINAIGRETTE

Though roasted beets are one of my favorite foods, their earthy flavor is an acquired taste. But this salad stands a strong chance of converting even the most hesitant beet eater. The sweetness of the roasted beets combined with creamy avocado and zesty mint is a magical flavor combination that's the perfect veggie-centric foil to all that pizza.

SERVES 6

1 pound beets, scrubbed and trimmed

Extra-virgin olive oil

Zest and juice of 1 orange (⅓ cup)

1 shallot, minced

1 teaspoon honey

Kosher salt and freshly ground black pepper

1 avocado, halved, pitted, and diced

¼ cup fresh mint leaves

Maldon sea salt

Preheat the oven to 450°F.

Place the beets on a large square of foil and drizzle with oil. Place another square of foil over the beets and crimp the edges of the sheets together to form a packet.

Roast until the beets are very tender (a knife should slide into the middle of the largest beet with no resistance), about 1 to 1½ hours. When the beets are cool enough to handle, slice them into wedges. Refrigerate the beets until chilled (they can be prepared the night before).

In a large bowl, combine the orange zest and juice with the shallot. Let sit for 10 minutes and then slowly whisk in the honey and 3 tablespoons oil. Season with kosher salt and pepper. Add the beets to the dressing, toss to coat evenly, and transfer them to a serving platter. Scatter the avocado and mint over the top, drizzle on a little more dressing, and season with sea salt.

PARMESAN-ROASTED CAULIFLOWER WITH GOLDEN RAISINS AND PINE NUTS

Cauliflower ditches its boring reputation in this addictive side that's bursting with juicy raisins, toasted pine nuts, and cauliflower that's roasted until it's as sweet as candy. This dish is great served at room temperature, so feel free to let it hang out on the table while you finish grilling the pizzas.

SERVES 6

¼ cup golden raisins

1 large or 2 small heads cauliflower, outer leaves removed and cut into bite-size florets

Extra-virgin olive oil

1 garlic clove, thinly sliced

Kosher salt and freshly ground black pepper

Wedge of Parmesan, for grating

Juice of half a lemon (1 tablespoon)

½ cup roughly chopped fresh parsley

¼ cup pine nuts, toasted (see page 47)

Preheat the oven to 400°F and line a baking sheet with parchment paper.

Place the raisins in a small bowl, cover them with hot water, and set aside.

On the baking sheet, toss the cauliflower with a drizzle of oil, the garlic, and big pinches of salt and freshly ground pepper. Spread out the cauliflower in an even layer and roast until it begins to turn golden brown, about 35 minutes, tossing once halfway through.

Drain the raisins and add them to the cauliflower, tossing to distribute evenly. Spread out the cauliflower in an even layer again and grate a fine layer of Parmesan over the top. Roast for 5 more minutes, until the Parmesan melts.

While the cauliflower is still warm, toss with the lemon juice, parsley, pine nuts, and another sprinkle of salt, to taste. Serve warm or at room temperature.

AFFOGATO

This two-ingredient dessert couldn't be simpler, but having the right equipment makes a major difference. I'm in love with my classic stove-to-table moka pot, which brews the dark espresso that Italians love . . . and its authentic look makes for such a pretty pouring experience.

SERVES 8

2 pints good-quality vanilla gelato

2 cups hot espresso

½ cup crushed espresso beans (optional)

Chocolate-Dipped Cherry Almond Biscotti (optional; page 153)

Scoop ½ cup gelato into each of 8 serving bowls or coffee cups. Pour ¼ cup espresso over each dish, and garnish (if desired) with a sprinkle of espresso beans.

Serve with biscotti, for dipping (if desired).

RESOURCES

Gatherings are much more fun to plan when you know where to look for all the little items that will bring your vision to life! These are the tried-and-true sources that have never let me down.

IN THE KITCHEN

Williams-Sonoma
http://www.williams-sonoma.com
I cannot walk into a Williams-Sonoma store without leaving with a couple new kitchen gadgets. Every item is designed with form *and* function in mind—a culinary hub for cooks of every skill level.

Sur La Table
http://www.surlatable.com
Anything your kitchen might ever need can probably be found at Sur la Table. Great dish towels; basic table linens in all colors; and every pot, pan, serving piece, and tool you could ever dream up.

West Elm
http://www.westelm.com
While this retailer is known mainly for furniture and home decor, I love shopping its kitchen collections for handmade baking dishes, utilitarian cooks' tools, and indie-made items such as Schmidt Brothers knives.

ON THE TABLE

Anthropologie
http://www.anthropologie.com
There are countless Anthropologie items gracing the pages of this book—it's difficult to name a spot that carries more beautiful, eye-catching, and downright special tabletop pieces! Just *try* perusing the housewares section in one of their stores without falling in love with some unexpected little piece.

Serena & Lily
http://www.serenaandlily.com
In addition to its beautiful furniture, Serena & Lily carries some of my favorite raw linen tablecloths, woven trays, and stoneware serving pieces. These are pieces you'll keep for years; they have that effortlessly elegant vibe that never goes out of style.

CB2
http://www.cb2.com
CB2 consistently astounds me with its incredibly affordable yet high-quality glassware and casual tabletop pieces. This is *the* place to scoop up extra wineglasses and appetizer plates before a big party without breaking the bank.

Newlywish
https://www.newlywish.com
When I want to add a special-occasion piece to my collection, Newlywish is the place to go. Their beautifully curated collection of fine china and serving ware from some of the most iconic brands around makes them a one-stop shop when you want to dress up the table a bit.

Terrain
http://www.shopterrain.com

Sometimes I just want to *live* inside Terrain. Its collection of highly edited items seamlessly merges the home and garden spaces, and I love perusing its organic, clean-lined tabletop pieces that are so spot-on for the naturalistic approach that I love.

Canvas
http://canvashomestore.com

The perfect mix of simple and extraspecial items make up Canvas's assortment of glassware, ceramics, serving pieces, and textiles. The company works with artisans around the world to create handcrafted designs that are as beautiful as they are useful.

Jamali Garden
http://www.jamaligarden.com

Jamali Garden is the little secret of florists, caterers, and event planners everywhere, since it seems to have just about every vase, candle, or ribbon you could need for a party at a fraction of the price of most stores. When I find myself needing a hundred hurricane lanterns or fifty yards of tulle, you can bet that Jamali is my first stop.

PAPER PRETTIES

Paper Source
http://www.paper-source.com

It's quite possible that Camille Styles, Inc., could singlehandedly keep Paper Source in business; it's our go-to spot for cardstock, envelopes, rubber stamps, wrapping paper, greeting cards, and just about any other paper prettiness we can dream up.

Antiquaria Design Studio
http://www.shopantiquaria.com

The gals at Antiquaria have their stamp all over this book—their calligraphy and custom-designed paper products are my absolute favorites, and when the occasion calls for something one-of-a-kind, you won't find a more individual or special source than this design duo.

Minted
http://www.minted.com

I've been ordering holiday cards and party supplies from Minted for years, and its offerings just seem to get better and better. Peruse its massive selection of options from independent designers around the world, and then choose the look that's absolutely perfect for your party (and let everyone *think* you paid for a custom design!).

ACKNOWLEDGMENTS

The best moments in my life are always accompanied by an overwhelming sense of gratitude to the people who've been part of them, and this project is no exception. From start to finish, I've been amazed on a near-daily basis by the talent, creativity, kindness, and generosity of so many, and this book is a product of our collective efforts. I feel so honored to get to share it with you.

First, to my photographer and friend Buff Strickland: You caught every vision I had for this book and brought it to life even more beautifully than I'd imagined. Trina Bentley, your design talents once again left me breathless, and made this book the visual escape I dreamed it would be. Thanks for making the process such a joy. Elizabeth Lewis and team, the natural artistry you brought to the flowers in each season blew me away. Chanel Dror, I couldn't have done it without your craftiness, creativity, and friendship. Jennifer Rose Smith, your imprint is on so many aspects throughout this book, but it shines brightest in your inspiration boards.

To my agent, Brettne Bloom: Since the day I started dreaming up this book, you've been my biggest cheerleader, co-strategizer, therapist, and partner in crime. Can't wait to see what adventures we conceive of next. A million thanks to Cassie Jones, my brilliant editor, who made this book smarter, sexier, and more "me" than I ever could have on my own. You are truly the best in the business. And to the entire William Morrow team—Megan Swartz, Kara Zauberman, Tavia Kowalchuk, Ashley Marudas, Amanda Kain, Rachel Meyers, Paula Szafranski, Anna Brower, Liate Stehlik, Lynn Grady, and Andrea Rosen—I feel so lucky to get to work with each one of you, and am grateful for all you've done to bring my dream of this book to life.

Endless gratitude to the many creative friends whose talents went into the making of this book: food stylists Ann Lowe and Meghan Erwin, Emma and Bailey of Antiquaria Design Studio, the Loot Vintage team, stylists extraordinaire Martha Lynn Kale and Mollie Morgan, Olivia Toepfer, Mia Carameros, and Word of Mouth Catering. Eve Tarlo and team: You guys are such pros, and I can't thank you enough for being there to capture the madness and turning it into a beautiful video. Andrea McWilliams, Carly and Clayton Christopher, and Lauren Cunningham: Your homes were the most beautiful backdrops for our tabletops—thanks for your hospitality. And many thanks to my friends at Anthropologie and Serena & Lily for your generosity in lending me the beautiful props that made my visions for each gathering come to life.

Adam: thanks for always believing in me more than I deserve; having you in my life gives me the courage to go out into the world and do things I never thought I could do. To my parents and parents-in-law, Chris, Ray, Jackie, and Gary: Your endless support means the world to me— you are truly the most loving people I know, and I hope I can grow up to be as generous and big-hearted as each of you. And of course to my darling Phoebe, my biggest inspiration and little love of my life: I'll always look back through the pages of this book and associate them with the first full, wonderful year of your life.

INDEX

Note: Page references in *italics* indicate photographs.